W9-COD-897

WHY DOES CHRIS DO THAT?

Some suggestions regarding the cause and management of the unusual behaviour of children and adults with autism and Asperger syndrome

by Tony Attwood

Dr Tony Attwood is a practising clinical psychologist who specialises in the field of Asperger syndrome. For the past 30 years he has met and worked with several hundred individuals with Asperger syndrome ranging widely in age, ability and background. He is the author of the acclaimed *Asperger's Syndrome: A guide for Parents and Professionals.*

THE NATIONAL AUTISTIC SOCIETY

First published 1993 by The National Autistic Society, 393 City Road, London EC1V 1NG

ISBN 1-931282-50-1

Designed and typeset by Column Communications

Contents

The Autism Asperger Publishing Company is proud to be the sole U.S. publisher of this book and a series of other carefully selected books on autism spectrum disorders originally published by the National Autistic Society (NAS) of Great Britain.

Other NAS titles published by AAPC include:
- *Asperger Syndrome – Practical Strategies for the Classroom: A Teacher's Guide* by Leicester City Council and Leicestershire County Council
- *Challenging Behaviour and Autism: Making Sense – Making Progress: A Guide to Preventing and Managing Challenging Behaviour for Parents and Teachers* by Philip Whitaker, Helen Joy, Jane Harley and David Edwards
- *Everybody Is Different: A Book for Young People Who Have Brothers or Sisters with Autism* by Fiona Bleach
- *It Can Get Better . . . Dealing with Common Behaviour Problems in Young Autistic Children: A Guide for Parents and Caregivers* by Paul Dickinson and Liz Hannah
- *The Other Half of Asperger Syndrome* by Maxine C. Aston
- *Teaching Young Children with Autistic Spectrum Disorders to Learn: A Practical Guide for Parents and Staff in General Education Classrooms and Preschools* by Liz Hannah
- *What Is Asperger Syndrome, and How Will It Affect Me? A Guide for Young People* by Martin Ives of the NAS Autism Helpline
- *Autism: How to Help Your Young Child* by Leicestershire County Council and Fosse Health Trust

NOTE:

British spellings and other conventions, including punctuation, have been maintained as in the original text. Some references have been updated and, by permission of the author, the term *autism spectrum disorders* (ASD) has been substituted for *autism*, where appropriate.

Foreword

After many years of advising parents and staff about Asperger Syndrome (AS) and autism (known collectively as autism spectrum disorders [ASD]), I have found that one of their most frequent questions is, 'Why do they do that?' followed by the more urgent question, 'And how can we stop it?' To answer such questions is not easy as, although we may have recognised ASD for over 50 years, we still do not understand its nature well enough to provide a comprehensive explanation for every unusual behaviour. However, we do know that children with ASD have certain features which clearly distinguish them from other children and my 20 years of clinical experience have taught me that any behaviour management strategies have to be modified to accommodate their unique disabilities. These differences are described in some detail in the hundreds of published research studies and the following sections will attempt to apply the results of these studies to explain why such unusual behaviour occurs and ways to encourage the person to 'do it less often' or at least to 'do something more appropriate'.

Before any effective management strategy can be developed it is necessary to establish the cause and the function of the behaviour. The first question you may ask in trying to discover the cause of any odd behaviour is whether the behaviour is due to ASD. The diagnostic criteria for ASD describe behaviours that are unique to the condition and can provide a means of explaining why people with ASD behave in such an unusual way.

The criteria for diagnosing autism change as our knowledge of the condition increases. The following sections will use the criteria of the American Psychiatric Association's *Diagnostic and Statistical Manual of Mental Disorders – 4th Edition-Text Revision*[1] (DSM-IV, TR, 2000), which would probably be the most universally accepted. The principal criteria are:

1. qualitative impairment in reciprocal interaction
2. qualitative impairment in verbal and non-verbal communication and imaginative activity
3. markedly restricted repertoire of activities and interests.

The following explanations and suggestions will also be relevant to children and adults with Asperger syndrome, a form of autism that usually occurs in association with normal intellectual capacity.

The criteria for Asperger syndrome are very similar to those for autism,[2] namely:

a) severe impairment in reciprocal social interactions
b) all-absorbing narrow interests
c) imposition of routines and interests
d) speech and language problems
e) non-verbal communication problems
f) motor clumsiness.

Qualitative impairment in reciprocal interaction

Most children have a natural ability to relate to their parents and other people from the moment of birth. Without any conscious effort infants recognise people as the most important components of their world. From very early in life there is a mutual understanding between parent and child and the feeling that they are on the same 'wavelength'. However, this is not the impression given by a child with ASD. There is the intuitive feeling that something is wrong with the child's ability to relate to other people from very early in the child's life.

There are a number of ways these impairments in reciprocal social interaction are shown. For the very young child there may be a marked lack of awareness of the existence or feelings of others. A characteristic that has been considered typical of ASD is avoidance of eye contact. However, it is not so much deliberate avoidance as not seeking mutual eye gaze at the start of an interaction or repeatedly looking at the face of the other person during the conversation or while playing.

People may have the impression they are being treated as an object and the child does not appear to really need people. There is a lack of that shared smile and sense of humour and when in distress the child with ASD is less likely to seek out or respond to comfort from an adult. Certainly the child seems unable to respond to love and affection to the degree one would expect. Although many normal children can be self-absorbed and 'cool', with ASD the severity of the problem is at a different and deeper level.

The pre-school child with ASD may not share activities with other children or adults, and the 'look at me' or 'look at that' actions are conspicuously absent.[3,4,5] In addition the child with ASD rarely copies the play of other children or spontaneously imitates their parents' domestic activities.

The school-age child with ASD invariably prefers solitary play or social play with much younger children and is not interested in joining in the social games of their peers. For example, during a conversation with a teenager with ASD, I asked him why he did not talk to the other children in the playground. His reply was, 'No thank you, I don't have to'. Clearly he had the ability to have a conversation with his peers but chose to play on his own in an isolated part of the playground.

An impairment in the ability to make peer friendships and an odd way of conversing with others is a characteristic of children with ASD of near normal intellectual ability. These children actually want to socialise but do not appear aware of the unwritten rules of an interaction or conversation. The child with ASD may approach an adult and start a conversation with a question which has no relevance to the immediate situation or the other person. For example, approaching a complete stranger without any initial social greeting and saying to them in a loud voice, 'What car have you got?'

The conversation may proceed by a series of questions and statements on a topic determined by the person, who appears unaware of any signals of surprise, boredom or embarrassment in the other person. The conversation is rarely modified to take into account the opinions of the other person or any interest in bearing about their experiences. At the end of the interaction the recipient of this 'monologue' feels the other person is very strange.

Those children with Asperger syndrome clearly want to socialise and are quite competent at maintaining a social conversation but they have considerable difficulty with intimate social relationships and social conventions. This problem with advanced social behaviour may not have become noticeable until the child was four or five years old. They may appear rude, naughty or inconsiderate but it is really that they are unaware of social conventions and how their behaviour may upset or offend other people. For example, while waiting at a supermarket checkout looking at the person at the till and saying to a parent (in a loud voice), 'Isn't she ugly' to which a hushed and embarrassed reply of 'You shouldn't say that' is met with the response, in a louder voice than before, **'But she is ugly'**.

The child seems very egocentric and lacks empathy, that is, appreciating things from another person's point of view. Such children are often indifferent to peer pressure at school and may not be desperate to have the latest clothes or toys. A question I often ask is 'What does the child do at lunch time when at school?' A consistent reply is that they are to be found in the school library or a secluded part of the playground.

The sequence of behaviours in a social interaction

When we interact with other people we have a recognised sequence of behaviours: looking at the other person, approaching them, making some greeting or comment, having a conversation and recognising the signals of when to end the interaction.

It appears that the incompetence in social interaction skills of a child with ASD can be due to an impairment at a particular stage in the interaction sequence. The most severely disabled may not acquire the first stage, which is to engage in reciprocal eye gaze or approach others. Some children make an approach but only for what the child wants, such as a drink, not to socialise. Some children with ASD are very motivated to interact with other people but may fail to give an appropriate greeting, such as 'Hello' or 'How are you?', and maintain the 'conversation' by a series of questions which are repeated even if the same answer is given time after time.

It seems as if the person's social behaviour has been recorded on to a record and the needle has got stuck, unable to progress to the next stage in the social interaction sequence. In contrast, the more socially competent child with ASD may have a more natural dialogue but may not appear to be aware of the appropriateness of a topic, when to stop talking about trains or butterflies, or how to end the conversation.

How can you improve social interaction skills?

It is important first to establish those stages the child has acquired and then encourage the acquisition of the next stage. If the problem is 'Why doesn't he look at me or come near me?' then encourage this first stage by linking the child's spontaneous gaze at your eyes with some socially enjoyable activity such as tickling, swinging around or a game of chase. Children then learn how to initiate an interaction and that an interaction can be fun, rather than an interruption of what they are doing.

It is essential to balance the 'I want you to do this' interactions with the 'Let's have fun together' interactions and underline the fact that such social play forms a significant proportion of your interactions with the child. This will encourage the child to spontaneously approach people more often.

If the child approaches others, then teach appropriate greetings; but do be careful. One greeting for the family may be a kiss but the child with ASD may not recognise who not to kiss, for example the postman delivering the mail. Should greetings not be given appropriately, how do you discourage a series of questions as the predominant form of interaction, for example?

First of all, this behaviour may be an echo of most of the natural conversational interactions initiated by adults to the child with ASD such as 'Why are you doing that?' or 'What's that?' Missing are the comments about some relevant activity or topic. This can be encouraged by ensuring your natural interactions include many comments, not questions, for example 'That car is going very fast' or 'That's a nice shirt'. If the child makes such comments spontaneously, then give some appropriate reply and interest.

Several experimental studies have demonstrated that typically developing peers can increase the frequency of social interactions for withdrawn children with autism[6,7] and AS.[8] The curriculum for a child with autism should include some time with typically developing children of the same age. Time spent with young normal teenagers can also provide extra social learning experiences. This can be achieved both in the classroom and in recreational activities such as sports and scouts.

One problem is that simple exposure to typically developing children will not automatically lead to an increase in social play. It is necessary to ensure the child is not on the periphery of events and knows the rules of the game: for example, when you're touched you chase after the other person, or when you receive the ball you pass it to someone on your team. This may be achieved via the guidance of an adult but when there is no supervision at break times, opportunities for social integration can be lost. However, I have found that the identification of one or two guardians can be very helpful. The guardian would be a class member who shows some maturity and interest in the child with autism or Asperger syndrome and becomes their partner in any games, shows them how to play and comes to their assistance or seeks help if they are teased or bullied.

At every opportunity consider how the activity could include a social component. For example, when the child has learnt to cook at school, he could prepare a meal not for himself but for another child, or when the biscuits are being shared around, pass the plate to each class member, saying their name and asking them whether they would like one (and learning not to be upset when they refuse).

Although the greatest rate of learning progress may be achieved by one-to-one sessions, remember that when the task is learnt, encourage the child to perform the activity in a group, taking turns and possibly even helping another child.

There are a number of effective techniques for social skills training which have been developed for those children with ASD who have the intellectual capacity to learn specific skills, including modelling, coaching and role play.[9] Tim Williams has described a very comprehensive approach for use with able children with ASD which also uses recreational games and direct instruction of what to do in specific situations such as 'Look at the eyes of the person you're talking to.[10] Simple feedback techniques can be used such as 'You looked at me and sat quietly while you spoke' and video filming can be used for modelling and practising conversational speech.[11,12] Another intriguing approach is that of Groden and Cautela.[13] They encouraged each of two children with ASD to imagine a social situation and linked this with imagining a pleasant event, for example, imagining playing with another child and then eating chocolate. The result was an increase in spontaneous social play.

Some children can achieve quite complex social interaction skills but can be either unaware when they make mistakes or hypersensitive to any criticism of their social competence. Such people may need counselling from someone who understands ASD and can help the person come to terms with the effects of their unusual disability on themselves and other people. They may also need to be told by their parents or teacher the specific rules of social conduct such as 'Just because you like computers does not mean you can walk into the neighbours' home to use their new one, especially if they have all gone to bed.'

For those with Asperger syndrome, school may be the only social life outside home and it may be necessary to actively encourage the person to pursue recreational and leisure activities with organisations such as scouts, local swimming or riding clubs, or special interest groups such as train spotters or collectors of stamps and coins, computer clubs or supporters of local sporting teams. I have found that the club member with Asperger syndrome is not necessarily the most eccentric person at the meetings.

The intellectually more able child often appears unconcerned about their lack of friends, but by adolescence genuinely wants to have close friendships. A method of improving skills and self-confidence is to have a social skills group for similar adolescents from nearby schools to rehearse appropriate social behaviour. These groups should include a majority of ordinary teenagers and include role play of situations such as asking someone to dance, coping with a refusal or discussing scenarios where someone has misunderstood social conventions. Margaret Dewey has described some appropriate scenarios for those with Asperger syndrome, such as going for a job interview, realising your hair looks a mess and asking to borrow a stranger's comb.[14]

The communication of feelings and thoughts

People with ASD find the world of emotions a foreign land. In the last ten years there have been an increasing number of studies which have examined perhaps one of the most important components of social behaviour, namely the communication of feelings and thoughts.

The studies on feelings have suggested that in ASD there is a dysfunction of the ability to comprehend and express certain emotions. Over the same period studies on the cognitive abilities of children with ASD suggest there is a dysfunction of the ability to appreciate what another person is thinking. Two theories have been proposed to account for the results of these studies, namely the Theory of Mind as proposed by Uta Frith and colleagues,[15] which is described by Simon Baron-Cohen as 'mind blindness,' [16] and the Theory of Impaired Affective-Cognitive Relatedness, proposed by Peter Hobson.[17] At this point I do not propose to discuss and compare the merits of these two theories and would refer the reader to the review by Anne Walters.[18] Here I propose to examine how the agreed deficits explain certain behaviours and what can be done to help.

Comprehension of emotions

The initial impression of a person with ASD is that they are indifferent to the emotions of others. Indeed they do have difficulty in interpreting emotional cues given in facial expression, gestures, posture or voice.[19,20,21] Thus one can never be sure that the person with ASD fully grasps the feeling that a person's face or action may express.

However, it is not true to say that they are totally indifferent, as the child with ASD may become very distressed by the emotional behaviour of other people. The problem is that the child with ASD may not know what the specific movements and vocalisations of another person mean, or how they are expected to respond.

This disability is shown in its severest form with the aloof child with ASD.[22] Here the child is distressed by the mere proximity of another person. The child is most at ease if one approaches in a very calm way with the absolute minimum of emotional content. A useful analogy is that of approaching a wild animal such as a deer that does not know whether your actions are friendly or predatory. With a very young aloof child with ASD it is helpful to approach the child in a very low key manner with slow deliberate movements, a calm voice and for only a few seconds. Once the aloof child is used to such low key, unemotional interactions you can very gradually increase the duration of the interaction and the emotional content.

We all have our own tolerance and expectation of the appropriate emotional behaviour of others; for example if the butcher unexpectedly came round the counter and gave you a kiss and huge embrace for having bought some sausages, the effect on you probably would not be a pleasant one. The ability to understand the emotional behaviour of other people is impaired in individuals with ASD and one practical application of this is that their tolerance of other people's emotional behaviour is at a much lower level than is often recognised.

It is important to pitch your emotional behaviour at a level the child understands and can cope with, for example, if the child has done well a brief 'Thank you' may be quite sufficient and enjoyed by the child. Any more demonstrative praise and the child becomes bewildered and may consider this an unpleasant experience. In situations where you may be angry with the child with ASD, being aggressive may make the child quite disturbed. As one mother said, 'If I get angry with him it only adds fuel to the fire.'

If you need to 'blow your top' leave the child and go somewhere else (perhaps into the toilet with the door closed), mutter relevant obscenities, then return to the child in a calm, assertive manner. On occasions where you show your love for the child you may have to be content with giving him a brief kiss or touch as any more emotional depth will cause him to withdraw and avoid such situations.

Expression of emotions

There have been relatively few studies of the ability of children with ASD to express emotions but the limited research data does support the clinical observation of a significant deficit in this area. Several studies have examined the ability of children with ASD to make faces expressing recognisable emotions and concluded children with ASD were less able than controls in assuming the required facial expression.[23,24]

A recent study examined the natural gestures of children with ASD and noted a conspicuous absence of gestures expressing interpersonal feelings such as consolation, love, friendship and embarrassment in situations where such gestures would be expected.[25]

Thus, it appears that children with ASD have a restricted 'vocabulary' of emotional expression. In practical terms this disability causes considerable distress to both the person with ASD and other people as the missing parts of the vocabulary appear to be those elements between a restrained and explosive expression, and those that require an appreciation of the feelings and thoughts of another person.

An intuitively appealing, but clearly imprecise analogy I use is to consider the feelings of the child with ASD as being expressed via a defective stereo amplifier. Some feelings are expressed only at maximum volume using a simple on/off switch. These emotions are purely personal such as frustration and annoyance.

Some feelings are expressed at minimum volume and these involve an appreciation or recognition of the feelings and thoughts of others. These emotions include affection, consolation and embarrassment.

Thus a minor irritation can trigger off quite a catastrophic reaction. The child can't open a door so she bites her hand, yet when she accidentally trips over and injures a classmate she offers no consolation, apology or sign of embarrassment. However, her brief touch of your arm or face may be the greatest depth of affection and love the child can express and is as precious as another child's embrace and 'I love you'.

There seems to be a lack of precision in the expression of emotions and an important point to remember is that the strength of the emotional expression of a person with ASD may be misconstrued. One able adult with ASD was considered as potentially very aggressive. This was because he would come very close to people and with a raised fist say, 'I'm going to punch you in the mouth' – a threat that he had never actually carried out. Understandably he had very few visitors. On investigation, it was clear he was simply agitated by the presence of new people but could not express his agitation in a more subtle and appropriate way.

However, he observed the actions and phrases on the television when people were angry and he found that the imitation of these actions succeeded in making people leave him alone. We had to carefully explain to visitors not to take a literal interpretation of what he said and that he could only express his feelings in a raw 'black and white' form.

Furthermore we had to teach him the alternative phrase 'Please leave me alone' which was equally effective but far more appropriate. A difficulty in precisely articulating or expressing feelings is noticeable when the person with ASD becomes distressed or agitated, and repeats whole sentences or conversations that may not be relevant to the immediate situation but may have previously been uttered by themselves or others at a time when a similar emotion was experienced. Here the message is the feelings, not the words.

A common question related to emotional expression is, 'Why does he laugh when I'm cross with him or when he's obviously upset?'

This paradoxical emotional response may be due to the difficulty that the person with ASD has with the expression of emotions. Laughter can be a tension release mechanism as in the phrase 'you either laugh or you cry'. I have known of an occasion when the sound of a child giggling hysterically was enough to wake his grandmother. On opening his bedroom door she realised he had been sick on his bed and was quite upset, but this was expressed as giggling, not tears or cries for help.

Sometimes the person with ASD finds a particular object such as a wasp or cardboard model provokes laughter. To the observer who doesn't see anything funny it appears almost as if the child is responding to voices in his head and there may be the suspicion of schizophrenia. However, it is simply that the child is anxious, for example in response to the danger of being stung by the wasp. Possibly the child may be recalling some previously humorous event associated with the object.

Sometimes just saying a particular word causes laughter, with some intensely personal humour associated with its pronunciation or meaning. This appears to be harmless – it's just a pity that we cannot share the joke.

However, it may mean the person is feeling anxious and that this is an effective tension release mechanism, not a perverted sense of humour or evidence of hallucinations.

One intriguing aspect of ASD that I have yet to explain adequately is when the child expresses aggression when affection was intended. One example was a little girl with autism who was gently caressing her mother's face and looked as if she was about to give her a kiss but then, suddenly, pinched her mother's cheeks. The little girl was then clearly upset for what she had done.

I have noted other occasions when the next level of greater affectionate behaviour was appropriate, yet aggression occurred to the distress of all parties.

Children with Asperger syndrome can also have problems with the precise expression of emotions. There is a tendency to 'jump for joy' when ordinary preschool children are excited. This appealing characteristic diminishes during the early school years but children and adolescents with Asperger syndrome may continue to jump and flap their hands when excited.

A characteristic that is of more concern for some adolescents with autism is the experience of sudden strong emotions, particularly fear and panic, that are quite out of proportion to the situation. Fortunately, these panic attacks can be helped by appropriate medication.

How can you encourage the comprehension and expression of emotions?

There are several ways a teacher or parent can develop a programme of activities that highlights the comprehension and expression of emotions. For young children with ASD, group activities in the classroom can centre on a particular emotion. Traditional songs can be modified such as 'You're happy and you know it' with specific actions such as 'Hug your friend'. In such games the teacher may initially have to model, prompt and reinforce those actions which express affectionate behaviour.[26]

For older and more able children with ASD a specific emotion such as happy, sad, angry, worried, love, can be used as the theme for projects using stories, music, drawing and role play. A fluency with words, gestures and actions which accurately describe feelings can be extremely helpful in later life, especially when someone asks the distressed person with ASD, 'What's happened?' They may then not just give you a description of events but also describe their feelings.

The curriculum should include material on how to recognise feelings in others and what to do. This can include role play of specific situations to teach the appropriate response, for example, when someone is crying, put your arms around them rather than stand and stare.

At home, parents can encourage the child to use certain actions such as a brief kiss on the cheek as a greeting or a thank you. These may be mechanical acts devoid of the degree of feeling one would wish, but it does teach an appropriate response for certain common social situations. This is particularly valuable as sometimes the disturbed behaviour of a person with ASD may be because they do not know what to do in response to the emotional behaviour of another person.

Try and identify those situations and teach appropriate safety actions or phrases such as: 'I'm sorry', 'Help me' or 'What should I do?' as these may enable both parties to understand each other.

Summary

The qualitative impairments in reciprocal interactions which are a unique characteristic of ASD are due to a lack of certain skills used in social interactions, and problems with the communication of thoughts and feelings. The main points to remember are:

1. Certain component stages in a social interaction may have to be taught, such as greetings.

2. Interactions with typically developing peers can be very helpful in encouraging the development of appropriate social behaviour.

3. There should be a balance between interactions which are instrumental, e.g. 'Do this,' and those which are pure fun.

4. Pitch your emotional behaviour at a level the child understands. This is often at a much lower level than you would use for ordinary children.

5. Some emotions are expressed very strongly but the child cannot express his feelings in a more subtle, precise or progressive way.

6. Those emotions which involve an appreciation of the thoughts and feelings of other people are often expressed in a mild way.

7. The child's 'vocabulary' of emotional comprehension and expression can be increased by specific activities both at home and school.

Qualitive impairment in verbal and non-verbal communication and imaginative activity

One of the earliest signs of problems with communication is the suspicion that the child is deaf, but closer examination shows the child's hearing range is normal. However, the child shows a lack of interest and response to the speech of others, and sometimes an indifference to their name being called.[27]

Some children with autism may start to say certain words before the age of two but these words disappear and the child becomes mute for several years or never regains their early speech. We do not know why this occurs but roughly 25% of children with autism do not acquire the ability to use speech.[28]

What is unusual about those who do not develop speech is that it is not compensated for by gesture or mime. Here the child may have to be taught alternative means of communication such as the use of sign language, symbols or pictures. Once this alternative means of communication has been learnt, the child with autism tends to restrict its use to achieving their immediate needs, rather than having a real conversation.[29]

In this sense the use of alternative means of communication is similar to the use of speech by those children with ASD who do become fluent speakers. These children may acquire speech at the normal age or several years later than expected but often fail to initiate or sustain normal conversational interchange. They have several unusual characteristics such as a repetitive and idiosyncratic use of language, saying 'You' or their own name when 'I' is appropriate, and have semantic/conceptual difficulties.[30]

This unusual language profile is also characterised by abnormalities of prosody, for example in pitch, stress, rate, rhythm and intonation of speech. This means that their speech is pedantic, lacks inflection, or has an unusual accent and abnormality of pragmatics, for example in turn taking, interruption of speaker, faulty use of gaze, and maintenance of conversation by questions. Here the conversational flow and exchange is affected. Thus although children with autism may learn to speak, when they do it is an odd form of speech. Although it may be effective to communicate what the child wants, there is a conspicuous failure to have an ordinary conversation with another person.

Children with Asperger syndrome usually develop very fluent speech, although they may be late talkers, and acquire an impressive vocabulary. Indeed, they almost become walking dictionaries, offering precise descriptions and definitions of obscure words. However, their speech is often characterised by a lack of modulation, an over-precise intonation and a tone that may not be modified to fit in with their peer group. One expects school-age children to change their accent to that of their friends, but I have noticed school age children with Asperger syndrome speaking with the regional or national accent of their parents although this was quite different to their classmates.

The person may also be able to use accurate and detailed scientific terminology, perhaps to describe the engine of a train, but find it hard to define the word 'embarrassed' or use it appropriately and in the right context.

Should the child have problems with their conversational skills, then speech and drama activities can help teach the art of good conversation. The content should include how to emphasise and augment the important words in speech. The drama activities can encourage expression and understanding of the feelings and emotional behaviour of other people.

A consequence of the unique profile of communication skills found in ASD is that the child may develop specific problem behaviours. The following section will examine verbal and non-verbal communication separately. It includes an examination of the impairment in imaginative activity in a broader appraisal of cognitive disabilities.

Verbal communication

A) Verbal comprehension

Not knowing how much of your speech a person with ASD understands can lead to frustration for both parties.

A simple but effective technique for use with all children with impaired language skills is to match the length of your instruction to the mean length of utterance of the child. Thus if the child speaks in one or two word sentences your instruction should be composed of utterances of a comparable length.

However, when this is applied to children with ASD, their propensity to repeat whole sentences perfectly (echolalia) may give a false impression of their level of verbal comprehension. The problem is that the child with autism may use the repeated sentence as the equivalent of a one word utterance without understanding that it is composed of individual words. The result is that the person with autism can be given instructions which are beyond their comprehension; the child becomes confused, fails and takes out her frustration on herself or her environment.

A failure to appreciate a person's level of verbal comprehension was apparent in the case of a young man with autism who had no speech and was notorious for his destructive behaviour. Careful observations showed this behaviour was triggered when he did not understand the spoken instructions of his care staff while doing his usual domestic chores. We found that if he was given one simple and short instruction such as 'Pour milk,' with prompts such as pointing and gestures, he was not only much calmer but he was also able to complete quite complex tasks such as preparing his lunch. This process required considerable patience and concentration from staff but succeeded in stopping his destructive outbursts.

The example above also highlights an important aspect of the acquisition of receptive language in people with autism, in that greater progress can be achieved when the training is linked to the teaching of daily living skills, where the person can more easily recognise the meaning and relevance of the words.[31]

Does this mean then that all your interactions with a person with autism should comprise simple phrases or sentences barking out orders like a sergeant-major? Certainly not.

There should be times when the person with autism can just listen to your speech without being expected to fully understand what you say. Much as a normal child likes to hear a story, there can be times when you are together, relaxed and almost 'write' the child a verbal letter. This allows the child to listen to speech as one would listen to music. A consequence is that the child with autism may achieve some enjoyment from listening to the sound of speech and some incidental progress in verbal comprehension and expression. It can also be a good social occasion, provided that the child is not forced to listen.

At the other end of the spectrum, those children with ASD and adults who acquire near normal levels of verbal comprehension unfortunately have a tendency to make a literal interpretation of what someone says. This leads to problems with common phrases and metaphors such as 'laugh your head off'. Do check if such a phrase causes distress and explain that it is just a 'figure of speech' not a scientific fact. It is possible to compile a list of common metaphors and provide an explanation of their intended meaning. Some modern cartoons also provide amusing misinterpretations of metaphors.

Sarcasm should also be avoided as this can cause confusion as to what you really mean.

B) Verbal expression

If you have a pre-school child with autism who is late to start to speak, obviously you will be keen to encourage them to acquire and use speech. The conventional methods used by speech therapists and teachers can be successful with children with autism, but there are two strategies that should be emphasised.

Some children may acquire their first words through singing, rather than in a formal language session.[27] Their first words may be from songs, advertising jingles or theme tunes used on the television. These could be incorporated into the language programme.

An interesting phenomenon reported by some parents and teachers is that although the child is usually silent, this may change under severe stress. For example, when being teased by a brother or sister, denied something they desperately want or when very angry, the stress may cause them to say complete words or phrases. You are left wondering if the child really said those words and hoping that someone else heard them or no one will believe you.

A mild level of stress may help the child utter the word. However, the emphasis is on mild. This is certainly not an encouragement to use draconian methods, as an inappropriate level of stress will lead to a tantrum and avoidance of similar speech therapy sessions. The approach emphasises determination, repetition and positive encouragement: in other words, no criticism for not being able to say the word.

For those children who develop speech, echolalia is a common characteristic. Echolalia, that is echoing a word, is a normal but brief stage in any child's development of speech. However, many children with autism do not progress beyond this stage, and may repeat single words, whole sentences or even conversations immediately after they have been heard or several days or even years later.

It was once thought echolalia was abnormal and had little constructive role in the acquisition of speech, and should be discouraged. However current opinion is that it has several useful functions. For the child with autism it may be their first use of spoken words or their only means of communication, and this has the obvious advantage of giving a speech therapist more material to work on than if the child were mute. It can also help maintain a dialogue when the child with autism has no other means[32] and, as echolalia is more likely to occur when the child does not understand what is being said, it can be a useful indicator of whether the child understands the message.

Finally, the child may simply enjoy the sounds of words and delayed echolalia may be considered a form of babbling. Therefore, it should not be considered as maladaptive or be discouraged.

One intriguing phenomenon I have observed is that some children develop a reasonable spoken vocabulary but use 'Yes' when 'No' was intended and vice versa. This is very confusing and can lead to great dramas. Therefore, in situations where the person says 'Yes' or 'No' and you respond appropriately and the child becomes very agitated, check that their intention was the same as their spoken word.

Another unusual characteristic is one which may be displayed by a child with autism who is distressed. This is the echoing of a phrase or even a whole conversation. The original phrase or conversation may have occurred some time ago in association with a similar emotion but have no relevance to the present context, for example, repeating 'Don't jump out of the window' when the child cannot go outside as usual because it is raining. Here it is important not to listen to the words but to recognise that the child – or adult – is having problems with an accurate verbal description of their feelings.

One form of verbal expression that may be rare for people with autism is to ask for help. The child or adult with autism then have a tantrum, not appearing to appreciate that other people may be able to help. Datlow-Smith and Coleman taught an adult with autism how to ask for assistance when having difficulty with his work. This significantly reduced his disruptive behaviour.[33] It may be necessary to teach a person with autism to say a safety phrase such as 'Steven needs help' or to use an equivalent sign on appropriate occasions.

This can be achieved by someone saying the phrase when the person with autism is having problems and needs assistance and then providing the help. For the person with autism this phrase serves to end an unpleasant experience and, if said early enough, may prevent an unpleasant experience for everyone. For those who have no speech, the same message can be written on a card.

At the other end of the continuum, some high-functioning children create their own words for everyday objects and events.[34] This may include totally new words, neologisms or idiosyncratic language such as that of a teenager with Asperger syndrome who always referred to ice cubes as water bones.

Children with Asperger syndrome tend to either talk too much or too little. It seems as if they do not identify or respond to the subtle signals that indicate it would be inappropriate to continue the conversation or monologue. The effect is as though the child has no 'off switch' for their voice. Another explanation has been provided by two adults with Asperger syndrome who discussed their incessant talking.

Anne: 'You know, I like the sound of my own voice because it keeps me from feeling lonely. I think there is also a little fear that if I don't talk a lot I may lose my voice. I didn't talk until I was almost five, you know. Before I started talking I noticed lots of things and now when I tell my mother she is amazed I remember them. I remember that the world was really scary and everything was stimulating.'

Jack: 'Talking to myself helps me figure out and practise how to express ideas well.'
(Dewey 1991, page 204)[14]

Anne appears to achieve some reassurance from hearing her own voice and Jack appears to vocalise his thoughts, perhaps as ordinary young children do, but this natural characteristic appears quite odd in an adult, who may be unaware or indifferent to how this makes them appear to others.

C) Non-verbal communication

Unless the child with ASD has some spontaneous communicative speech by the age of six years, the chances are communicative speech will not develop.[35,38] For such children the inability to use speech to convey thoughts, feelings and needs will obviously lead to frustration. This frustration can turn to anger and often results in a child whose behaviour is considered unmanageable or disruptive.

For those children with autism who are unable to acquire an effective vocabulary of spoken words, non-verbal means may be acquired. Various sign systems have been developed with some success in acquiring an effective means of communication and even encouraging speech.[36]

Unfortunately, some children with autism fail to respond to sign systems. Do not become despondent as some success has been reported using symbols, pictures, written communication, and electronic keyboards.[37-41] No one system appears to be universally effective but at least there is a choice.[29]

For those people with autism who have little or no speech, or alternative forms of communication, disruptive behaviours such as aggression and tantrums can be used as a means of communication.[42] These behaviours can translate to such comments as, 'I don't want to do this', or 'Leave me alone', 'I'm bored', 'I don't understand', or 'I'm frightened.'

Such behaviour can be very effective in obtaining the desired response. Once the behaviours have been recognised as a means of communication then alternative means can be taught using appropriate signs or words.[43,44] I would add that an effective means of communicating 'No' or 'Leave me alone' may be a useful starting point.

D) Cognitive disabilities

The unique communication impairment in ASD may be a consequence of an underlying social and cognitive disability. At this point it is worth reviewing the relevant research on cognition (i.e. knowing and thinking) in order to explore how deficits in this area may explain certain behaviours.

Many people with autism are of below average IQ so they will naturally have difficulty with learning, but they may also have specific cognitive disabilities due to autism. It is necessary to be aware of these particular disabilities and to adapt the child's curriculum to accommodate them.

The following sections will describe the specific cognitive disabilities, and how they may affect the child's behaviour and learning.

Stimulus over-selectivity

An analysis of error patterns in training exercises has shown that severely intellectually-disabled children have a propensity to attend selectively to one restricted source of information and to exclude others. This characteristic also appears to occur in children with ASD.[45]

This means that the child may attend to one feature which may not be the relevant one. For example, they may look at the shape of a picture card or jigsaw piece, not the picture itself, or concentrate on your hand as you demonstrate something, not the activity itself. In addition the child with ASD may look at tiny details such as the colour of someone's eyes rather than focusing on their face.

The problem is the child may 'lock onto' one stimulus and not switch to others. For example, you may show the child a picture of a cat and a house, and upon request she learns to point to the cat. However, you may be unaware she is using the tail to identify the cat, and when pictures of another cat and a dog are presented she is totally confused. Thus you have to ensure that the child attends to the relevant cue, uses simple material with no distracting or irrelevant details, and repeats the activity with a variety of different examples.

Cross-modality problems

A common activity with young children is to encourage them to listen to a word and then point to the corresponding picture or object, or to say the appropriate word that describes the picture. In these tasks the child has to use two different senses at the same time.

Children with ASD have specific difficulties co-ordinating information between the auditory and visual and tactile senses.[46] This may explain their relative failure on certain activities but they may achieve more success with activities which predominantly use one sense, especially the visual.[47] Thus there may be greater progress with simple visual matching activities such as posting boxes, picture or shape lotto and dominoes.

Sequencing

People with ASD seem to have difficulty with sequencing, that is, working out what happens next.[48] The child may have learnt each of the stages in using the toilet but cannot link them all together and in the right order, for example, wetting pants after going to the toilet.

When a problem in sequencing has been identified, it is necessary to provide temporary prompts of what to do next, which can in time be faded out as the links are learnt. People with ASD are more relaxed when they know what is going to happen next because they find unpredictability and chaos unbearable.

You can help by providing a simple schedule of the sequence of activities expected over a given time.[49] For example, at home have a series of pictures or photographs which describe what is going to happen during the day, such as breakfast, teeth cleaning, car journey to shops, returning home and making lunch. At school the sequence of desk top activities could be prepared in a series of boxes: when the work in one box is finished, take the items from the next box.

This procedure can also be used for teaching a sequence with domestic chores and work routines and can use real objects, e.g. having the broom next to the clothes pegs which are next to the window cleaning spray.

The child's need to know what happens next is illustrated by the case of a young child with ASD who was very anxious to know when her mother was due to return to pick her up from school. Verbal reassurance was of no help but we succeeded by placing a photograph of her mother on the classroom clock at the time when she was due. The child then recognised that her mother would return when the hands reached the photograph. Giving a clear indication of the sequence of activities or when something will occur can have a significant effect on reducing agitated behaviour due to the natural level of unpredictability or chaos in the life of the person with ASD.

Imagination

When identifying autism in a child, one of the positive indicators is a poverty of spontaneous imaginative or symbolic play in relation to the child's mental age.[50]

25

However, this unique abnormality in the child's play may not be a failure of acquisition but a failure to use such skills.[51] In practical terms this means that trying to engage the child with autism in pretend play means choosing an activity with which the child may have considerable difficulty. It may be necessary to start with elementary imaginative activities on the lines of 'What else could you do with this?' and, where practicable, to use real objects as opposed to miniature or highly representational toys.

The social play of ordinary children includes a range of imaginative and 'let's pretend' games, from dressing up and tea parties to playing the teacher or policemen and robbers. The child with Asperger syndrome may find such games difficult to comprehend and be part of. They may require some tuition in what is required as they may be confused as to whether the game involves reality or pretence. It may help to teach an appropriate safety phrase for situations of uncertainty over what to believe, such as 'Are you pretending?' and if the reply is yes, not to take it seriously.

Many children with Asperger syndrome prefer to read information books rather than adventure stories but it is possible to encourage flexible and imaginative thought processes by classroom activities of 'Let's suppose that...' or 'What's silly about...?' and some children can achieve quite novel and interesting replies.[52]

Generalisation

Once an activity has been learnt, children with ASD often fail to transfer their learning to other situations.[53] Skills taught at school may not be spontaneously carried out at home or in another classroom and vice-versa. This is infuriating for staff and parents who may argue that the child's failure in another environment is due to some inadequacy on the part of other people. This can develop into a mini-'civil war' between the various agencies.

We do not clearly understand why a lack of generalisation is so pronounced in ASD but, once people are aware that it is likely to occur, then steps can be taken to help. Close co-operation and communication are required with regular opportunities for various parties to see what the child can do and how it is achieved. Parents need to visit the school or adult centre and staff need to visit the home. No one person will have a monopoly on success and records of progress and techniques must be maintained.

Generalisation can also be encouraged by group teaching and deliberately teaching the activity using different settings and people.[54]

Perceptual abnormalities

At times, the behaviour of children with ASD has a resemblance to that of partially sighted and deaf children and many children with ASD are at first thought to be deaf.[55] However, it is not that the children with ASD have sight or hearing deficits, but that they are unable to make sense of what they see or hear.[47] In other words, they are unable to encode stimuli meaningfully.

Further research which has been reviewed by Frith and Baron-Cohen has confirmed that lower-level processing of sensory information is relatively normal, as shown in the ability of children with ASD to echo stimuli, but this production of an almost perfect 'copy' indicates a limited ability to recode sensory stimuli.[56] This recoding is dependent upon being able to perceive any stimulus as organised in a particular way, and to identify the salient and redundant components. It is here that children with ASD have problems.

Thus, when teaching a particular activity it is important to clearly isolate and simplify the relevant features. Children with ASD may therefore need a more detailed task analysis of the individual stages or components of an activity than other children with intellectual deficits.

Studies of the perceptual abilities of children with ASD have suggested that they may have a disability in using imagery.[47,57] For example, the child with ASD may have problems 'picturing' the absent object or action you are miming or incorporating an imaginary object in his gestures.[58] The implications of these studies have not yet been fully explored but this information should be remembered when teaching a manual sign system. It may also account for a slower rate of progress of some children with ASD when learning certain signs.

Imitation

Children with ASD have a deficit in the ability to imitate and rarely do so spontaneously.[59,60] Motor imitation, which develops quite early in normal children with a minimum of encouragement, is difficult for children with ASD to acquire. They may observe how someone does something such as opening a box and then repeat the same actions to achieve the same end for, example, getting a biscuit.

However, what is usually missing is copying the actions of other children or adults to be like them, to be part of the group, or to be like mummy, daddy or the teachers.

However, there is one intriguing aspect of the response of the child with ASD to people imitating them that can be very helpful. Dawson and Levy found that having an adult imitate the behaviour of the child with autism significantly increased attentiveness, eye gaze and exploratory play.[61] The explanation may be that this procedure made the behaviour of adults more predictable and under the child's control so that the child could relax and achieve greater concentration. This technique can be especially useful with very young and withdrawn children.

Kinaesthetic cues

If a child with ASD is not as good at learning by imitation as other children, what techniques could help teach him how to do things? One sensory system and means of exploring the world at which children with ASD seem to excel is movement. The child may spend many hours exercising his fingers by flapping and tapping and his limbs, for example, by using the swing or trampoline.

This natural interest in the sensation of movement can be used to help the child learn various motor actions. The approach is to physically move the child's limbs or fingers through the activity so that the child learns from kinaesthetic cues.[62] I have found this 'hands-on-hands' teaching has been very effective with many young and severely delayed people with autism. This can involve tracing the child's fingers around a shape or physically guiding her hands and limbs when teaching dressing skills.

Indeed, some children may be more likely to succeed if you do not use visual cues, where you expect imitation following your demonstration, or verbal cues, that is expect comprehension of your spoken instructions. Instead try to initially manipulate their fingers and hands through the activity so that the child gets to feel what to do. This approach is also applicable to children and adults with Asperger syndrome.

Temple Grandin is a scientist who as a child was diagnosed as having autism, although with modern diagnostic criteria, Asperger syndrome would be more accurate. She has written her autobiography and several articles on the experience of having ASD. In one article she writes:

'Even as an adult I find it easier to learn about something if I can actually do it instead of watching.'[63]

This information may be extremely helpful for teachers who find the child has problems learning from spoken instructions.

Memory

People with ASD have specific verbal and visual memory difficulties.[64] While long term memory may be good, memory for recent events can be poor. This may explain why some questions are repeated after the answer is given. It will help to have all relevant material for a task within view of the person and, for those who can read with meaning, to have written instructions to refer to.

Motivation

One of the most exasperating parts of working with children with ASD is their apparent lack of motivation to concentrate on the constructive task you have prepared, in contrast to a very strong motivation to engage in their own repetitive activities. Why do children with ASD seem to have less motivation for certain activities?

A normal person's degree of motivation is based on various desires or drives such as the need for approval, affection or personal gain and the desire to compete, succeed, conform and imitate. The person with ASD does not seem to have these drives, hence their poor motivation. The drives they have seem to be to succeed in completing a task and to engage in repetitive, often solitary, activities.

When this feature is transferred to a learning situation, it means that the usual motivators and rewards in the classroom are going to be less effective. Nevertheless it is possible to use certain types of rewards to increase motivation. An Autism Reinforcer Checklist has been developed and it is extremely useful as a means of compiling a list of those activities the person with autism finds enjoyable.[65] The main categories are:

- edible, e.g. chocolate, raisins, potato chips
- social, e.g. tickling, wrestling, chasing, praising, hugging
- material, e.g. a mirror, balloons, blocks
- activity, e.g. going for a walk, water play, swings, time alone, flushing toilets.

Access to each reinforcer would be earned by completing the task.

However, I would add a few comments from my experience of using such reinforcers.

Edible reinforcers can be a problem in terms of being impractical or difficult to administer. The child may be more interested in grabbing the food than doing the task. Moreover, these rewards are very artificial and you do not always have them with you.

Social reinforcers such as praise and affection need to be within the tolerance of the child (see chapter on 'Impairment in reciprocal interaction', page 7). An enthusiastic hug may be quite startling for the child with ASD but an appropriate level of social praise is far more natural and easy to provide.

Material rewards could include access to items for self-stimulation such as a piece of string, set of keys, etc. It may be considered a bizarre reward but if it is the only thing that motivates the child with ASD use it. I have found that the use of such rewards has not led to an even greater demand for access to these items and there is now some research evidence to support use of this type of self-stimulating material as a reward.[66,67]

Activity rewards are useful, especially at the end of a session. They may include allowing the person with ASD to be alone or to ask questions on their favourite topic. On this occasion he has 'earned' the opportunity for such indulgence. Children with Asperger syndrome often have a high degree of motivation and achievement in their specific area of interest, but often have poor concentration in other areas. It is important to have a flexible curriculum and to incorporate the special interest in the activity, for example, using an interest in flags to teach geography or an interest in clocks to learn about fractions.

More able adolescents and adults with ASD may have motivation problems for personal hygiene and domestic chores. Such lethargy is also common with normal adolescents but they may be 'persuaded' by a dislike of being embarrassed and will occasionally do things to please parents – or to stop them nagging. Adolescents with ASD are not so easily persuaded and may be less aware how their appearance and personal hygiene affects other people.

A mercenary but effective approach is to use money as an incentive: if you clean your teeth, you can have 10 pence, your room cleaned, 50 pence. This cash buys access to the child's obsession such as magazines that have circuit diagrams or train tickets. This procedure is similar to a token economy or report card system which has been used with able teenagers and adults with ASD in the work environment.[33]

Improving the child's competence in the learning situation

Several research studies have looked at how to increase the performance and learning of children with ASD. Most of this research has been done on very young and severely affected children with ASD but the basic principles hold for those who are older and more able.

The following are guidelines to remember during any learning session:

1. Obtain the child's attention. Call their name, clap your hands, do anything to ensure the child is attending to you or the activity.

2. Choose tasks which can be completed within the child's attention span. If their attention span is a second or two, use brief tasks such as one bead on a thread. The child with ASD may have difficulty maintaining a prolonged gaze at the task material but a brief glance can be enough for the child to take in the requirements.

3. Allow time for the child to think before he responds. Some children with ASD are impulsive responders.[68] They may have to wait for two or three seconds before starting.

4. Maintain concentration. This can be achieved by phrases such as 'Keep looking' and if necessary acknowledge any attempt perhaps with a 'Thank you' or 'Yes'.[69,70] Some children with ASD naturally use peripheral as opposed to central vision. If this is the case it may not be wise to force the child to look directly at the activity.

5. Do not comment upon failure, just show the correct way. The word 'no' or any criticism or comment on failure can make people with ASD very agitated. If the person has made a mistake, just show the correct way. Any comment like, 'No, that's not the way' is likely to inflame the situation and lead to avoidance behaviour.

   Children and adults with ASD have a very low tolerance of frustration and often develop disruptive or non-compliant behaviour to avoid or end learning activities associated with frustration or failure. It is possible to reduce such behaviour by simplifying the activity, avoiding criticism and making reassuring comments.

   This obviously applies to those with limited intellectual abilities but children with Asperger syndrome can also become extremely agitated if they fail a task and can abandon a project or course of study in response to an ordinary level of criticism. They also seem to need more than the usual degree of reassurance.

6. Errorless learning. Try and maximise the chance of success by ensuring the task is relatively easy to complete. Remember, nothing succeeds like success and a high rate of errors often leads to disruptive behaviour.[39]

7. Upon success, start the next activity straight away. After the intrinsic reward of success, quickly move on to the next activity while the child is in a good mood.

8. Use a variety of activities in the same session. A range of different activities can be used in one session which will maintain motivation and attentions.[71]

9. Minimise distractions. Children with ASD have difficulty in filtering out irrelevant sensory information. This means that extraneous noise or movement can confuse the child. Sometimes silent 'hands on' teaching is the most successful, perhaps choosing a time with as few other people around as possible, or working in a quiet separate area.

10. Initially choose activities that are relatively easy for children with ASD. Children with ASD find some activities particularly difficult, (see section on cognitive disabilities page 34) but they are relatively more proficient with sensory/motor tasks such as matching shapes, and pictures.

11. Continue using physical prompts. Once an activity has been learnt, one would assume there will be no further problems. I have noticed that many people with ASD can acquire a particular skill but occasionally seem unable to start the activity. It is almost as if they have problems 'getting their brain into gear with their body'. When the person knows what to do but this time seems unable to get started, a physical prompt may help get them going. It is almost as if your gentle push of the person's hands towards the first action gets their body 'into gear'. Thus, even after the activity is learnt, you may still have to use the occasional physical prompt.

12. Motor co-ordination problems. Although children with autism can appear very agile, with gross motor skills such as running or climbing they can have poor co-ordination problems, especially when using their hands.[72] Co-ordination problems also occur in Asperger syndrome with a very noticeable clumsiness and poor co-ordination which can be seen when imitating the actions of others and balancing.[73] Should such problems be apparent in the classroom or sports activities then remedial programmes can be designed by an occupational therapist or physiotherapist.

Remedial therapy may improve co-ordination and reduce the degree of clumsiness but sports such as football and cricket should be avoided as the person's poor co-ordination is conspicuous. Alternative sports which rely on accuracy, for example, darts and ten pin bowling, may be more appropriate.

Summary

A lack of appreciation of how much a person with ASD understands and can achieve will lead to frustration for both of you. For the person with ASD this frustration may be expressed by disruptive behaviour. An understanding of the unique communication and cognitive skills found in ASD will significantly reduce the intensity and frequency of such disruptive behaviour.

The main points to remember from this section are the following.

Verbal comprehension

1. Match the length of your instruction or comment to the average length of utterance of the child.

2. To increase motivation, link communication training with the teaching of daily living skills.

3. There should be times when the person with ASD is expected just to simply listen to your speech, much as a normal child will listen to a story or music.

4. Beware of confusion due to a literal interpretation, e.g. 'Cry your eyes out'.

Verbal expression

1. Echolalia should not be discouraged.

2. You may have to teach the person how to ask for assistance when they are having difficulty with a task.

Non-verbal communication

1. Some children with ASD respond well to communication using manual signs, symbols, pictures, and electronic keyboards. No one system is universally effective but there is a choice.

2. Disruptive behaviour can have a communication function, indicating messages such as 'I don't want to do this' or 'I need help'. Alternative means of communicating the same message can be taught.

Cognitive disabilities

Stimulus over-selectivity
1. Ensure the child attends to the relevant cue.
2. Use simple material with no distracting or irrelevant details, and repeat the activity with a variety of examples.

Cross-modality problems
1. More success may be achieved with activities which predominantly use one sense, such as shape lotto.

Sequencing
1. Provide temporary prompts of what to do next.
2. Pictures can be used to describe the sequence of events.

Imagination
1. Where practicable, use real objects, not imaginative or highly representational toys.

Generalisation
1. Children with ASD often fail to transfer their learning to other situations.
2. Have good communication between all care givers.

Perceptual abnormalities
1. Clearly isolate and simplify salient features.
2. Undertake a detailed task analysis of the activity.

Imitation
1. Imitating the child's behaviour can increase attentiveness and exploratory play.

Kinaesthetic cues
1. Manipulate limbs and fingers through the action i.e. 'hands-on-hands' teaching.

Memory
1. Have all relevant material for a task within view.
2. Those who can read may benefit from having written instructions to refer to.

Motivation

1. Compile a list of those activities the person with ASD finds enjoyable.
2. Access to self-stimulation and repetitive activities can be an effective reward.
3. More able people with ASD can respond well to a token economy or a report card system

Enhancing performance in the learning situation

1. First, get the child's attention.
2. Choose tasks which can be completed within the child's attention span.
3. Allow time for the child to think before responding.
4. Maintain concentration e.g. 'Keep looking'.
5. Do not comment upon failure, just show the correct way.
6. Ensure the task is relatively easy to complete.
7. Upon success, start the next activity straight away.
8. Use a variety of activities in the same session.
9. Minimise distractions of sound and movement.
10. Initially choose activities that are relatively easy for children with ASD, particularly sensory/motor tasks.
11. You may have to use occasional physical prompts to start the activity
12. There may be a need for a remedial programme to improve motor co-ordination.

Markedly restricted repertoire of activities and/or interests

This aspect of ASD has been neglected by research yet it can make life almost unbearable for parents. There seem to be three features associated with this diagnostic criterion, namely simple repetitive actions, the development of elaborate routines and a preoccupation with a narrow range of interests.[74]

1. Simple repetitive actions

One of the characteristics which is most noticeable in young children with ASD or those who remain severely intellectually-disabled is their propensity to engage in repetitive self-stimulatory actions such as rocking, twirling objects or flapping their hands and fingers. These actions appear to have no constructive use other than to provide some sensory stimulation. The child seems almost 'mesmerised' by the action and, if adults did not intervene, this behaviour would virtually occupy their whole day.

These actions seem to be maintained by some intrinsic sensory consequences, i.e. the child enjoys them; but they can also occur in response to frustration or increased stress or anxiety. The level of repetitive actions increases when the person with ASD is unsure of what to do, experiencing too many demands or distractions, or is tired. Conversely, the level of repetitive actions reduces in conditions of success or peace and quiet.

I sometimes use the amount of repetitive play as a 'barometer' to indicate the amount of stress experienced by the person with ASD. Thus there may be two functions of such behaviour: first, it may be that the activity is enjoyable for its own sake and, second, it may be a response to stress or anxiety.

But what can you do to stop these actions occurring so often?

A number of techniques have been successful. For those actions which provide some 'enjoyable' sensations, try and think of a more acceptable sensory alternative, for example, for rocking encourage the use of a swing or trampoline.[75]

Indeed, simply providing a variety of sensory experiences appears to reduce the motivation to engage in repetitive actions.[76]

A simple but effective approach is to divert the person to some other activity, perhaps some simple domestic chore or a social interaction between you and the child. One young man with autism at an activity centre caused a problem with his tendency to rock backwards and forwards when he should have been planing a piece of wood. The manageress was intimidated by the sight of this tall man who was so entranced in his rocking that she was afraid to interrupt him. We explained that she simply had to say in a firm voice 'Alan, stop rocking,' in order to break the trance, and then add 'Start planing' to give him an alternative action. This use of a terminating instruction followed by an alternative action can be quite effective.

A recent study encouraged several more-able children with ASD to reduce their level of repetitive behaviour by drawing a mark on a piece of paper after a specified interval without engaging in any repetitive actions. These marks could later be exchanged for various rewards.[77]

In my opinion it is important that there should be occasions when the person with ASD can engage in his repetitive actions without interruption – a form of 'free play'. However, you may have to teach the person to wait for those occasions or that they are not acceptable in certain situations such as at a meal table but are allowed in others such as in the bedroom or garden, or when the task you have given the person is finished.

The approach of establishing a compromise of when and for how long the person can indulge in repetitive play can actually reduce the desire or compulsion for such behaviour. From the point of view of the person with ASD, if they do not know when the next opportunity will arise to twiddle with a blade of grass or find a toilet brush, then they will take every available opportunity to gain access and may be unable to think of anything else until this is achieved.

With a technique known as 'controlled access', i.e. a known period of waiting, as well as some distracting constructive activity, and the guarantee of subsequent access, the child's desire can be reduced. The time period between access to the activity depends on the individual but this gradually increases to perhaps only several times a day.

When the person with ASD starts a repetitive action in response to some frustrating event, there are several points to remember. The level of repetitive actions diminishes when the person with ASD achieves success or can comply with demands. Therefore apply the principles described in the previous section on cognitive disabilities and non verbal communication.[78,79]

The level of repetitive actions also diminishes in environments that have a low level of distracting sensory stimulation, such as fewer decorations on the walls and the presence of familiar people.[78,80] So it is worthwhile taking a careful look at the physical and social environment of the person with asd to minimise the effects of these factors.

2. The development of elaborate routines

People with ASD prefer structure and predictability in their daily lives and appear to develop routines and rituals to make life predictable. However, if such routines are disrupted there may be an intense emotional reaction, which could be misinterpreted as a temper tantrum but is really more like a panic attack.

Variety is not the spice of life for the person with ASD: they are happiest if they can maintain the same pattern in their daily lives. Chaos and uncertainty are unbearable. One interesting component is that a minor change in an established routine will produce a severe reaction, for example a chair in a new position or a new route to school, whereas there is an acceptance of moving house or a new car.

Once a sequence of events has occurred in the same pattern on several occasions for the person with ASD it must occur that way again. Over time there tends to be a gradual extension in the number of actions in the routine. For example, he has to touch a particular item of furniture before he will get into bed. This then becomes two items, then three and so on, with perhaps the addition of turning around once, then twice – until a simple activity takes ages.

Why do these routines occur and why do they gradually take up so much of the person's time?

The answer may be that they are performed to make life predictable, i.e. to impose order as novelty, chaos or uncertainty as to what happens next seem intolerable to the person with asd

Jerry is a man with autism who said of his childhood, 'nothing seemed constant, everything was unpredictable and strange.'[81] The research literature offers some support for this hypothesis in that people with ASD have been noted to fail to become accustomed to novel stimuli and have a limited capacity to process novel information.[82,83] In addition, an application of the Theory of Mind as applied to ASD is that, if the person cannot determine what another person is thinking, then the behaviour of other people must also be very unpredictable. Thus they may insist on the same routines to avoid any new or unexpected situations, especially social situations.

The problem becomes one of living with someone who cannot tolerate change and whose rituals are taking an increasing proportion of their daily life. We had an example with a young man who could dress himself independently but took an hour to do so, due to the number of times he had to take off and put on each item of clothing and stand on his bed and touch the ceiling of his bedroom. He became very disturbed if this routine was interrupted.

One aspect of these rituals is that they are learnt behaviours; in the previous section on 'generalisation', reference was made to the tendency by the person with ASD not to repeat the same behaviours in new settings. It appears that the person with ASD uses certain environmental cues to 'trigger' the routines. If these cues are removed, the behaviour may be avoided. Using this hypothesis we decided the young man should go into the bathroom to be dressed in the morning and in this new environment he was dressed in five minutes and firmly encouraged to go downstairs for breakfast before he could start any new rituals.

The previous example involved changing the behaviour by changing the environment which was associated with the behaviour. Another approach is to avoid that first cue that triggers the routine. For example, in the case of a child who rigidly followed a set routine when entering his home after school, we recognised that going through the front door was the cue which triggered the sequence. The problem was solved by the child entering the house by the back door. He then had no anticipated sequence and therefore no determination to complete his routine.

Unfortunately, sometimes it is just a 'battle of wills' between the two of you as to how much of this behaviour will be tolerated. The person with ASD must have limits set on their routines and the limits must be applied consistently. For young children with ASD who have not yet developed elaborate routines it will certainly help if you deliberately include some degree of variety in the child's daily life so they learn to be more tolerant of change at an early age.

3. A narrow range of interests

In early childhood the person with ASD seems preoccupied with activities which provide sensory stimulation or satisfaction, such as flapping fingers in front of their eyes, sifting sand, spinning or tapping objects, consuming as much food as they can find or taking a drink whenever they see water or a tap. Those who have severe intellectual deficits may not progress from this stage, but more able children progress to more complex interests as their intellect develops.

The next stage seems to be the development of an intense 'attachment' to a particular object or class of objects which are collected at every opportunity and must be in close proximity to the child. These objects can be quite ordinary, such as keys, or extraordinary, such as bath plugs or plastic buckets. If the object is in view, the person with ASD has an almost desperate need to obtain the object and is quite distressed if it is taken away. This degree of attachment may appear to be stronger than any attachment to parents. The attachment may last several months or years, only to be replaced by other types of objects such as clocks or vacuum cleaners. When several examples of the same item are available they may be manoeuvred into lines with the same objects often placed in the same position, such that a line of toy cars looks like a traffic jam.

The third stage occurs in those children who develop speech and comprises an intense fascination with a particular topic. Instead of objects being collected the person collects information on topics such as means of transport, astronomy or electronics. For example, an eight-year-old child with Asperger syndrome was fascinated by the national football league and knew an extraordinary amount of information about the number of goals scored by a team or individual players, results of matches over the last five years, team positions within the league and could repeat sections of commentaries on games. However, when encouraged to actually play the game at school, he remained stationary on the pitch but gave a continuous commentary on the play. He had no interest in actually playing the game or competing.

The common themes in these interests is the presence of straight lines and symmetry as in circuit diagrams, flags or drawing buildings, or order as in bus timetables and arithmetic calculations. An illustration of this fascination with lines and order occurred in a conversation I had with a teenager with autism who had not developed speech but who could communicate by typing sentences using an electronic keyboard. I asked her about any special interests when she was a child and she typed the words 'telegraph poles'. I asked 'Why, telegraph poles?' and she typed 'Totally wonderful symmetry'. Her comment was most illuminating, and many children with autism of all levels of ability do appear fascinated by symmetry. This may be the reason why many children are determined to ensure all the doors and drawers in a room are closed or open.

The specific interests may come and go, lasting months to decades, and it is impossible to predict when they will change or what will replace them. The level of skill that is acquired can be quite impressive, yet the person with autism seems indifferent to any admiration.

A fourth stage can occur during adolescence and beyond, whereby people with ASD develop an intense fascination with a particular person who may be fictitious such as Dr. Who or someone they know. They appear to have an adulation of the person, wanting to know all about them. The adulation is quite intense and of concern to parents due to the young person's lack of awareness of social conventions. As with previous interests, this adulation is all consuming for a while, then ultimately replaced with adulation for another person.

The content of these interests seems to change for no apparent reason but one interest is always replaced with another. When asked for advice on a programme to end a particular interest I am always concerned that the intense fascination is very resistant to normal reward and discouragement programmes. In addition, the replacement interest is invariably determined by the child and may be more of a problem.

The daily life of a person with ASD often may not include the range and depth of pleasurable experiences that other people have. However, their particular interest may be one of their few pleasures, so a more successful approach might be a compromise of where and when the activity is allowed. Some interests can be used constructively, such as an interest in sniffing shoes channelled to a programme to clean them, an interest in machinery channelled to working with contract gardeners mowing lawns and an interest in flags used by the teacher to teach number work, for example counting flags instead of cubes. The answer may be to try and think of a constructive application of the interest and to allow the person some private time to indulge in their interests when it does not upset other people.

Some repetitive interests of those people with a severe intellectual disability can be dangerous or socially unacceptable. In such cases, a programme will have to be designed to reduce the behaviour. The programme should include several elements, namely:

- encouragement to undertake other activities as a form of distraction
- trying to redirect the behaviour into more acceptable ways, e.g. playing with the hair of a doll rather than of other children
- it may be necessary to have some means of discouraging the behaviour when it occurs.

It is also important to recognise that repetitive behaviour increases when the person is under stress. The cause of the stress may be a change in routine, lifestyle or expectations, or too much noise, chaos or social activity. Such behaviour is also more likely to occur when the person is tired, for example at the end of the day, or bored.

The programme can be more successful if it helps the person cope with these unavoidable causes of stress by having a sanctuary where the person can go when agitated or suggesting an activity that requires a lot of energy; in other words to 'burn up' feelings of agitation or distress. More information on this approach will be given in a later section.

Summary

Although we recognise that people with ASD have a markedly restricted range of activities and interests, this is one aspect of ASD we know the least about in terms of cause and management. The following are simple suggestions that are mainly based on experience rather than objective research.

Simple repetitive actions
1. Try and find a more acceptable alternative means of stimulation e.g. using a trampoline or providing a variety of sensory experiences.
2. Divert the person's attention to some other activity.
3. Have a compromise as to where and when such actions are acceptable.
4. Freedom to indulge in repetitive actions can be used as a reward, especially for those children who have little motivation for anything else.
5. Such behaviour reduces when the person achieves success and has a low level of distracting sensory stimulation.

The development of elaborate routines
1. Try and identify the trigger that initiates the routine and if possible avoid the trigger.
2. A change of environment may allow you to stop a routine, for example changing bedrooms.
3. Sometimes it is just a battle of wills to stop the child engaging in their routine but you must be consistent.
4. For young children, ensure they get used to change in their life.

A narrow range of interests
1. You may have to compromise as to where and when the person may pursue their interest.
2. Try and think of a constructive application of the interest.
3. Programmes can be designed to reduce the behaviour using distraction, encouraging similar but more acceptable actions and a better means of coping with stress, tiredness and boredom.

Abnormal perception of sensory stimuli

The previous sections have used the current diagnostic criteria as a means of explaining why the behaviour of children with ASD is qualitatively different to other children. As we learn more about ASD the diagnostic criteria change and currently there is a suggestion that there should be a new criterion which describes the unusual responses of children with ASD to sensory experiences, particularly sound and touch.

Edward Ornitz refers to a disturbance of sensory modulation – that is under-reactivity and over-reactivity to sensory stimuli and Coleman and Gillberg refer to abnormal sensory responses, especially to sound.[84,85] A precise definition of this criterion has yet to be agreed, but an abnormal perception of sensory stimuli by ear, eye or touch is noticeable in children with autism even before the age of three years and in children and adults with Asperger syndrome.[86,87]

This abnormality appears to have an effect on one or several sensory modalities where ordinary sensations are perceived as extremely intense or extremely weak. Unfortunately, there have been conspicuously few research studies of this extraordinary aspect of ASD and few theoretical models.[88] Nevertheless, some of the most illuminating descriptions of this phenomenon are provided by children and adults with ASD describing how they perceive the world.

The perception of sounds

Certain sounds can be quite upsetting for some children with ASD. It is quite common to observe children with ASD with their fingers pressed tightly over their ears, presumably to shut out specific sounds or a volume level which is upsetting. The following quotations of people with ASD provide an explanation of what the child may be experiencing.

'I was also frightened of the vacuum cleaner, the food mixer and the liquidiser because they sounded about five times as loud as they actually were.'

'The bus started with a clap of thunder, the engine sounding almost four times as loud as normal and I had my hands in my ears for most of the journey.'

'Another trick which my ears played was to change the volume of sounds around me. Sometimes when other kids spoke to me I could scarcely hear them and sometimes they sounded like bullets'. (Darren) [89]

'While I was typing the capital I in the last sentence, the dog scratched and her collar jangled so I heard a crashing painful noise.' (Lucy, personal communication)

'I was living in a world of daydreaming and fear revolving about myself. I had no care about human feelings or other people. I was afraid of everything. I was terrified to go in the water swimming, [and of] loud noises.' (Tony) [90]

'What do children with ASD hear? Sometimes I heard and understood and other times sounds or speech reached my brain like the unbearable noise of an onrushing freight train. Noise and confusion of large gatherings of people overwhelmed my senses.'

The autobiography of Temple Grandin refers to her sensitivity to noise.[91]

'Intensely preoccupied with the movement of the spinning coin or lid, I saw nothing or heard nothing. People around me were transparent. And no sound intruded on my fixation. It was as if I were deaf. Even a sudden loud noise didn't startle me from my world. But when I was in the world of people, I was extremely sensitive to noise.'

An unusual sensitivity to noise was also included in a description of Jerry.

'According to Jerry his childhood experience could be summarised as consisting of two predominant experiential states: confusion and terror. The recurrent theme that ran through all of Jerry's recollections was that of living in a frightening world presenting painful stimuli that could not be mastered. Noises were unbearably loud, smells overpowering. Nothing seemed constant; everything was unpredictable and strange.'[81]

Further references to a sensitivity to certain sounds are found in the other reports of first-hand accounts of ASD.[92]

Clinical observations often suggest that children with ASD can be unduly upset by sudden, unpredictable sounds such as a dog barking, specific sounds such as certain electrical appliances, leaves rustling in the wind, or the speech of other people, particularly in noisy social gatherings.

Many children and adults with ASD have a fear of unexpected noises such as the starting of a vehicle engine, a telephone ringing, or another child shouting. One adult with ASD who had always had a fear of dogs said it was because she could never tell when the dog was going to bark. Another child was referred because of his strong avoidance of his father and panic if he came near. Careful observation showed he could not tolerate the noise of his father coughing; unfortunately his father had a chest problem which caused frequent coughing.

Another example is of a young girl with ASD who was coping very well in her classroom but, for no apparent reason, would become very agitated. On observation I noticed her agitation was always in response to other children standing up and moving their chairs. I realised the noise of the chair scraping against the floor was unbearable for her.

Other children have had a panic reaction to the noise of electrical equipment such as the vacuum cleaner, or to the clashing of cutlery. A young man with ASD lived in a hospital for people with learning disabilities and was referred because he refused to eat his meals and was rapidly losing weight. Watching him at meal times I was conscious of the noise level, particularly of crockery and cutlery being placed on tables. I asked that he remain after everyone had eaten and they had left the huge dining room. I gave him the lunch he had previously refused and now, in a quiet empty room, he visibly relaxed, eating all his lunch and more.

Some children with ASD become very distressed in response to natural sounds, such as a wave breaking on a beach, leaves rustling in the trees, or rain on a roof. A suitable analogy of what it may feel like is the natural phenomenon of discomfort many people have to specific sounds such as the noise of fingernails scraping down a blackboard. Perhaps the perception of the person with ASD of some common sounds is comparable, so no wonder they can be severely distressed, especially when they do not know how to stop the noise and no one else perceives it as so unbearable.

The previous comments of Temple Grandin and others suggest that the volume of other people's speech may sometimes be misperceived by children with ASD. It is well known that one of the first indicators of autism is suspected deafness where the child does not seem to respond to the speech of others. However, it also appears that some children may be over-sensitive to the volume of speech of others or themselves. It is intriguing that some children with autism only speak in whispers yet can speak with normal volume when requested to.

Another interesting phenomenon is those few people with ASD who speak in an artificial way. One man spoke in a very high pitch. When I asked him why, he replied 'I don't like the sound of my voice', but he could tolerate his falsetto voice.

How to identify which sounds are perceived as very intense

Clearly the child who puts his fingers to his ears in response to a certain noise wants to avoid that sound, but on other occasions careful observation is required to examine whether a specific sound precedes agitated behaviour. Sometimes behaviour such as jumping over the school fence and running off can be an attempt to avoid the noise and chaos of the school playground. If the child remains in the playground when on their own and it's quiet, then the presence of noise from other children may be a factor. Sometimes it is helpful to compare the child's behaviour in quiet and noisy circumstances to establish whether there is a significant difference between the two environments.

I sometimes wonder if some children with ASD who intermittently scream or hum are not only playing with the sounds but also using this as an attempt to screen out those environmental sounds they find unpleasant.

The perception of touch

Some children with ASD cannot tolerate being lightly touched by another person or specific tactile sensations. The term which describes this behaviour is 'tactile defensive'.

Temple Grandin has the following description of her reaction to touch.

'I pulled away when people tried to hug me, because being touched sent an overwhelming tidal wave of stimulation through my body. Small itches and scratches that most people ignored were torture. A scratchy petticoat was like sand paper rubbing my skin raw. Hair washing was also awful. When mother scrubbed my hair my scalp hurt.'[93]

'Church was a nightmare because the petticoats and other Sunday clothes itched and scratched. The good clothes felt differently than everyday clothes. Whereas most people would adapt to new clothes in a few minutes, it took me three or four days to adapt. Many behaviour problems in church could have been avoided by a few simple clothing modifications. Changing types of underwear is still a problem today.'

'The reason I wore shorts during cold weather was because I could not tolerate the feeling of long pants against legs which had been bare all summer.'[94]

Some young children with ASD are notorious for their avoidance of wearing clothes or only wearing specific garments. This behaviour can be acceptable in a child under two but when older this can be quite a problem, especially when the child has learned to remove their clothes when no one is watching and at a speed to be recommended to the *Guinness Book of Records!*

For some children with ASD there can be screams because of having to sit on a particular surface, such as a wooden bench, sand or grass. The child may be exceptionally responsive to tickling but hate a gentle stroke on their arm at bedtime. Light and gentle touch may be abhorrent to the child with ASD but rough and tumble play and squeezing fairly firmly may be accepted and even enjoyed.

Temple Grandin built herself a 'squeeze machine' which provided 'deep pressure stimulation' using foam rubber and pressure over a wide area of her body. This may explain why some children with ASD like going under sofa cushions and mattresses or being held tightly by blankets at bedtime.

A hypersensitivity to touch is fairly easy to recognise and it is possible to desensitise the child by gently stroking them with different textures and encouraging them to engage in the tactile activities they avoid. Deep pressure stimulation can have quite a calming effect and one way of achieving this is by rolling the child up in a mat. Sheela Ram has described how a duvet or quilt can be used to calm some children with ASD when they become very disturbed.[95] Obviously this technique should be used only to calm the child, and not as means of punishment or imprisonment while you go away and do something else.

Some children who are 'tactile defensive' may also have an abhorrence of the texture of certain foods. This is not the normal stage of childhood of stubborn refusal to chew or eat vegetables, but when the child appears to have a genuine panic reaction to specific foods: their face goes white, their heart rate goes up and they are desperate to avoid the food.

A confusing factor is that children with ASD tend to avoid novelty and one problem is that parents are intent on providing a good and varied diet. This leads to a conflict of interests: predictability versus variety. Here the situation is frustrating for both parties, although the child is not as terrified as when they seem to perceive specific oral sensations as extremely unpleasant.

The intolerance of specific food textures is very difficult to treat. The confrontation approach where the child is forced to eat the feared food is to be avoided and gentle persuasion can be more effective, for example camouflaging small amounts in accepted food, eaten when the child is relaxed or distracted.

Visual perception

An abnormal response to visual stimuli occurs with some children with ASD but it may not be easy to recognise. The following comments from Darren explain how he perceived some objects and situations.

'I used to hate small shops because my eyesight used to make them look as if they were even smaller than they actually were.'

'I also remember one Christmas when I got a new bike for a present. It was yellow. I would not look at it. Extra red was added to the colour making it look orange, and it blurred upwards making it look like it was on fire.'

'I also couldn't see blue clearly, it looked too light and it looked like ice.'[89]

One young man I know was asked about any sensitivity to visual material and replied: 'I am scared to see colours, they flow together, they are so blinding to me. If I twist my fingers in my eyes I want to go mad.' Several others have referred to how their eyes 'hurt' when they see certain types of lights, especially light from neon tubes, or there is a change in illumination.

I noticed an example of distorted visual perception in a child who visited a roller skating rink. On approaching the concrete rink, he refused to step forward, touching the rink as though it was water. Another reference to a distorted visual perception is provided by Darren, who referred to a trip to Bristol Zoo, writing 'my eyesight blurred several times that day and once I could see no more than a yard in front.'[89]

Some children with ASD have the intriguing habit of giving the impression of having difficulty in recognising the things they see while some appear to recognise the food before them by smelling it first. The problem is that the observer does not perceive the object or situation in the same way so this phenomenon can only be inferred from the child's behaviour.

If a distorted perception of visual stimuli is suspected then the child needs reassurance and help to overcome the understandable fear or panic reaction (see page 49).

The perception of aromas, pain and temperature

In the description of Jerry's recollections of his childhood, he said he found smells overpowering.[81] One of the common characteristics of ASD is a fascination with smelling objects and people, but it appears some aromas can be quite upsetting to the child with ASD. When observing a child who has unpredictably disturbed behaviour I sometimes make a note of any aromas present, such as perfumes and disinfectants. I subsequently check whether the disturbed behaviour recurs when a specific aroma is re-introduced.

An unusual response to pain is often noticed when the child suffers a minor injury and does not appear to flinch or be upset, for example when a wooden splinter is lodged in their skin or on drinking a very hot drink. Although this may seem to be one of the few advantages of having ASD, it does mean the child is prone to bruises, cuts and tissue damage because he or she has not learnt to avoid certain activities. This may lead others to think the child is abused or neglected.

This higher pain threshold can also lead to problems when the child is given a smack, the child with ASD appearing indifferent to this form of punishment. To obtain a response from the child, parents may resort to several very hard smacks. This method of punishment with a child with autism – or any child – should be avoided or used with extreme caution as it could lead to an injury – and suspicion of child abuse. It may also teach the child to do the same to others when frustrated or wanting to stop some activity. Moreover, smacking can leave parents feeling guilty for being so brutal.

Finally, some children with ASD seem to have a different internal 'thermostat' and can go outside in bitterly cold weather and object to wearing warmer clothing or wear layer upon layer of clothes on a hot summer's day. Conversely some children appear very sensitive to minor fluctuations in temperature, becoming very hot or cold for no apparent reason, when everyone else feels quite comfortable.

Assuming the child is not going to get frostbite or collapse from the heat, and is not suffering from an illness, it may be best to just accept this as one of their little eccentricities and in time we may discover the reason.

Management of the fear or panic reaction

Once you have identified which sound, object, situation, texture or aroma is perceived as unbearable, what do you do to overcome the child's fear or panic?

First of all, the child needs reassurance and an opportunity to calm down – certainly not criticism or threats. One way of encouraging the child to calm down is to take them out of the room or situation, avoiding the stimuli causing the panic reaction. Then provide them with some distracting activity such as a simple domestic chore.

Another approach is to 'burn up' tension by vigorous activities on the swing or trampoline, or going for a walk. When the person has calmed down, you can return to the previous setting, but do remember to return to the same activity so the child does not learn that if he 'throws a wobbly' he can avoid doing what he doesn't want to do.

If the problem is a sensitivity to certain sounds then it may be possible to use ear plugs, the industrial headphones used with noisy machinery, or a 'walkman' to play the person's favourite music. I have found the use of music to be the most successful approach.

An alternative approach is to constructively use the means of the person with ASD for blocking out unpleasant sensations. Temple Grandin writes, 'Today, even as an adult waiting in a busy airport, I find I can block out all the outside stimuli and read, but I still find it nearly impossible to screen out the airport background noise and converse on the phone. So it is with children with ASD. They have to make a choice of either self-stimulating like spinning, mutilating themselves, or escape into their inner world to screen out outside stimuli.'[91]

Thus, when a child with ASD becomes extremely agitated because of an abnormal perceptual response to sensory stimuli and cannot be reassured, comforted or helped to avoid the source of the problem, then he or she should be allowed or even encouraged to engage in their favourite repetitive or obsessional activities as their effective means of screening out the stimuli.

If the problem is tactile defensiveness, there are a number of therapy activities to reduce this sensitivity to certain types of touch. These include rubbing the skin with different textures, massage, vibration, deep pressure such as an obstacle course of crawling between mats, sleeping in a sleeping bag and vestibular stimulation, for example using a swing, rocking chair, etc.[96]

An occupational therapist can be helpful in providing advice for individual children.

The next stage in management and prevention of the fear or panic reaction is to identify the specific 'triggers' for the behaviour. These may be specific such as sitting on a particular carpet, aroma, or visual stimuli such as a specific object or situation. There may be some simple practical solutions to avoid the situation, such as fabric at the end of a chair leg to prevent the scraping sound when the chair is moved.

But what about those situations you cannot avoid, such as a child who has a fear of house plants?

This was the case with one child, who did not have a level of speech to explain why he was so terrified of these innocuous objects. Our approach was to treat the fear much as one would treat the fear of ordinary people who have phobias. The fear of certain objects is quite common: many people fear snakes, spiders, rats, etc. If people require treatment to reduce the fear response, they undergo a programme to desensitise them, which involves graduated exposure to the feared object or situation. Thus if you feared spiders, you would be encouraged to relax – the opposite of fear – and think of a dead spider some distance away, maintaining the relaxation. Gradually you would become accustomed to thinking of and eventually being close to larger spiders, until your fear reaction has gone.

This approach has been tried with children with ASD.[97] For the child with the fear of house plants, we chose a time when he was relaxed, namely at the end of the day and after his bath. We gradually got him to accept a very small house plant, initially at the other end of the room, then on a table beside him.

This procedure reduced his fear response. However, we encountered a problem common to some children with ASD, described in the section on cognitive development, namely the inability to generalise. His mother explained this quite succinctly by saying, 'He gets used to the one you train him on but any new plant makes him go berserk.'

Nevertheless there has been some success associating laughter with the feared object, for example by tickling or offering something nice to eat such as ice cream.[98,99] A successful approach is that of having the child first observe you with the feared object or in the feared situation, such as the shower cubicle, then you patterning the child through the activity and finally the child accepting the situation on their own.[97]

However, there has been remarkably little research in designing and evaluating treatment programmes to overcome the fear or panic reaction of the child with ASD.

Summary

Some children with ASD have an unusual response to sensory experiences which seem unremarkable to other people. Sudden sounds or a noise level to which we easily become accustomed can lead to severe distress. Other children with ASD cannot tolerate specific textures or gentle touching of their bodies, and some appear to misperceive objects or situations so that they seem unbearable. Even ordinary aromas can be overpowering and the child can appear anaesthetised to low level pain or indifferent to heat or cold.

If this is one's perception of the world, no wonder a child with ASD may display quite bizarre behaviour. A major problem is identifying which environmental stimuli trigger such distress where the response may be panic, odd behaviour such as fingers pressed against the ears or repetitive self-stimulatory behaviour to block all outside stimuli.

The following approaches can help.

1. Make a note of any consistent sound, tactile stimulation, object, situation or aroma that precedes any agitated behaviour that is obviously not due to frustration, change in routine, poor social skills, etc.
2. Some sensory experiences can be avoided, for example, by going to another room or selling the food mixer; others may be reduced by introducing:
   - a barrier e.g. earplugs, headphones
   - temporarily allowing the child to engage in self-stimulating activities to block external sensory experiences.

3. To reduce the fear or panic reaction, the child may respond to a programme to be desensitised to the feared object or situation. This may be achieved by introducing a low level of the feared situation but ensuring the child now experiences a pleasant emotion, such as relaxation or eating chocolate or having someone show them that the object or situation is not as bad as they fear and providing support and reassurance.

Is the behaviour typical for the person's age?

In normal child development we acknowledge the specific behaviours typical of certain ages, and that children's preschool years and adolescence can be the most exasperating for parents. The description 'terrible twos' refers to highly mobile, fearless toddlers who are determined to have their own way and want immediate gratification with an apparent inability to be quiet. These characteristics may continue until children are three or four years old but by the time they go to school they are much more civilised and rational – although I am of the opinion that some 'normal' adults never really grow out of this stage. Adolescence is another period when we anticipate and endure behaviours such as prolonged periods of self-pity, rebelliousness and determination to be independent.

We have all experienced these behaviours and stages, and there is much common and scientific knowledge on what is normal for a particular age. However, we know less about how these natural stages affect the behaviour of children with ASD and whether the behaviour we are concerned about is due to ASD or simply typical of the person's age.

During the pre-school years the unusual behaviours of children with ASD seem at their most severe, with social isolation, repetitive play, resistance to learning, and hyperactivity at a peak. Many parents wonder how on earth they will manage to live with the child if this is how he will behave for the rest of his life.

Experience has shown that this is only a stage, and between the ages of six and twelve there will probably be a period of significant progress. The child becomes more responsive to classroom routine with an increase in attention span and improved self-care skills. For those with an intellectual disability the development of a means of communication helps to reduce the level of frustration and frequency of temper tantrums and the child often becomes less resistant to social approaches by adults. With guidance the person can also learn elementary social interaction skills. Obviously these improvements are relative to the child's behaviour in the preschool years and level of intellectual disability but in general it is a time when the child's behaviour tends to improve.

For those children with Asperger syndrome, the pre-school years may not have been unusually difficult and at primary school the child may show steady progress. Nevertheless, adolescence is a potentially difficult time for all children, but especially so for those with ASD. The normal problems of adolescence will include mood swings, the desire to be autonomous yet not having the necessary skills and increased sexual drive. The natural mood swings may include periods of withdrawal, lack of appetite and motivation.

These changes in mood may be due to hormonal fluctuations which will eventually stabilise. The desire to be autonomous will include being more determined to have one's own way. The difficulty here is that the person's size and strength may be equivalent to an adult but their competence and understanding may be equivalent to a child. The adolescent with ASD may quickly realise his strength can work to his advantage. Parents and staff may feel they are vulnerable and unable to control some situations. Physical restraint and threats of consequences may only escalate the situation and increase the risk of injury or damage.

The best approach is to adopt an assertive, non-aggressive manner. I have watched small and fragile teachers control the physical outbursts of towering adolescents with ASD by giving a firm instruction such as 'sit down,' with their posture and tone of voice giving every indication that they will not tolerate such nonsense and that they are in control. The key is the teacher's confidence and determination – not making reference to the disruptive behaviour and giving a simple command to get the person doing something else. However the foundations for such an approach will have been laid down much earlier in the life of the person with ASD.

Any management technique used in childhood must be equally applicable when the person has the size and strength of an adult. Gary Mesibov has expressed this succinctly in the question 'Can I do this technique if the child is bigger than me?' If not, use a different approach.

An increased interest in sexual activities may not be accompanied by an awareness of the appropriateness of certain behaviour and its effect on others. The adolescent with ASD may have to be told where and when specific behaviours are allowed because there may be no appreciation of how his behaviour may cause embarrassment for other people.

Adolescence is the bridge between childhood and being an adult and the school curriculum may need some revision at this time. Traditional educational activities may have limited relevance to the person's prospective adult lifestyle and there should be greater emphasis on:

1. improving independence skills e.g. cooking, washing laundry and personal hygiene
2. familiarity with community facilities e.g. shopping centres, restaurants and public transport

3. the development of recreational interest e.g. swimming, gardening and contact with a wider social group, e.g. joining a local sports club
4. social and vocational programmes.

Previous sections have referred to the limited ability of the person with ASD to cope with change and it is extremely important not to subject the adolescent with ASD to major changes in lifestyle, routine or support networks as, at this stage, their coping mechanisms may be at their least effective.

The person with ASD may not be a prospective candidate for university but may have physical strength equal to his age peers and be motivated by activities where he can easily see the relevance and end product of his work. The curriculum thus has less emphasis on intellectual pursuits and more on practical activities.

The above problems are an extension of those found with ordinary adolescents yet adolescents with ASD may have additional problems.[100] The hyperactive child often becomes a hypo-active young adult. Where once he would not sit still, he now has little energy for any activity. The solution is to examine the daily activities of the person and introduce more age-appropriate activities, particularly those that increase independence and require some physical exertion.

Those with Asperger syndrome or with near normal IQ may show an increased interest in forming friendships, yet they may be very naive in social situations. There can be a new desire to be like other people and initial attempts at having a boyfriend or girlfriend relationship. However, when they are with their new 'friend', they often maintain the social conversation with a monologue, ignoring the experiences and opinions of the other person, yet can also be very hurt if ignored by others.

Their competence in social situations appears to be learnt, and is often an imitation of other people so that in novel situations they may not have a clue what to do. A young man with autism brought his girlfriend home from his sheltered workshop but, as he had never observed what to do in such a situation, he left her downstairs to talk with his mother while he concentrated as usual on his electronic circuitry in his bedroom. He was totally unresponsive to the embarrassed silence between his mother and his new girlfriend. In contrast, his poor social skills were less conspicuous at the workshop as he imitated the courtship of the other workers. The family had further problems in that he did not know what he was doing wrong and saw no reason to talk to his girlfriend in his own home.

Those people who acknowledge being different to others can become oversensitive to any comment on their social inadequacies. This may be followed by a period of total denial that they are different to other people. However, they may become quite depressed over their inability to have intimate personal relationships and develop a very low self-esteem. One problem for parents of adolescents with autism or Asperger syndrome is their vulnerability to social, sexual and financial exploitation. Parents may have to maintain their guardianship role for longer than with neuro-typical teenagers.

Clinical experience and research has suggested that about one-third of adolescents with autism are affected by a significant deterioration in skills and behaviour. This may last only one or two years, or the whole of the teenage years.[101] The person with autism may regress to an earlier developmental level, lose some academic skills and exhibit an increase in disturbed behaviour. There may be no apparent environmental cause such as changing schools or separation of parents and we have no way of predicting which children have the potential for deterioration after puberty. We do know, however, that deterioration is more common with girls.[100]

One in six children with autism have epileptic seizures diagnosed in their pre-school years but a similar proportion have their first seizure during their adolescence.[102] The most common type of epilepsy is complex partial seizures.[103] This is widely accepted as the form of epilepsy in which behaviour problems and aggression are most likely to occur. During a seizure the person's behaviour may initially appear quite odd with specific motor actions such as chewing or running, followed by intense feelings, particularly fear and rage. The person cannot be consoled or distracted, but eventually returns to their normal self. Throughout the process they may not have lost consciousness. Severe self-injurious behaviour such as head-banging, skin-gouging or self-biting has been associated with complex partial seizures which originate in the frontal lobes of the brain.[104]

An illustration from my own experience is a girl who was referred for extremely disturbed behaviour, including self-injury, in specific situations, especially the school playground. From observations it was clear the behaviour was not a deliberate act to avoid certain activities and was out of proportion to the situation. She was experiencing extreme distress that was not directly attributable to a psychological cause. A referral to a neurologist and subsequent investigation confirmed the presence of complex partial seizures of fronto-temporal origin and the behaviour ceased with the administration of appropriate anti-convulsant medication.

If extreme fear or aggression occurs, to self or others, in the absence of external precipitating factors such as frustration, and if this is very intense but of short duration, then an examination by a medical specialist is warranted, as there are effective means of treating epilepsy in people with autism.[102]

About one in three adolescents with autism go through a temporary – one or two years – or prolonged period of regression. However, the majority continue to achieve significant progress and some, particularly those of normal IQ, can show substantial improvement.[105]

Eventually adolescence ends and, although there have yet to be adequate longitudinal studies, my clinical experience and that of others suggests that the mid-twenties onwards is often a time of progress.[106,107] Even those adolescents who showed deterioration after puberty usually show a significant improvement in their late-twenties. The improvement seems to be a greater tolerance of change and an increased interest in people. Furthermore, there is a noticeable showing and accepting of affection to others, particularly parents, and an increased interest in being self-sufficient.

The higher the IQ, the better the prognosis, as the person seems to use their intelligence to learn how to relate to other people, but it is essential to have a supportive family, to explain what you should and should not do and to provide reassurance and acceptance. Many children with Asperger Syndrome desperately want to be like other people during their adolescence and may be quite depressed by the effects of their disability. However, by their twenties they seem to come to terms with their disability and receive great enjoyment from their work or special interests.

As adults, the majority of those with Asperger Syndrome become less conspicuous, a natural part of the rich tapestry of life.[108] Unfortunately a small minority may develop psychiatric symptoms and require appropriate treatment.[109]

How to identify the cause of the behaviour

The previous sections have described a number of reasons why a person with ASD can behave in a way so unlike other children. In summary, the main reasons are:

1. impaired competence with specific skills used in social interactions
2. deficits in communication and thinking
3. strong motivation to develop routines and a restricted range of interests
4. an abnormal perception of sensory stimuli.

When someone with ASD becomes agitated there are likely to be several reasons operating at the same time. For example, a child may bite his hand because he has just failed to complete a task and does not know how to communicate 'I need help'. The noise level in the room is becoming unbearable and the teacher's face has changed but the child does not know what the signals mean. The only form of communication and emotional expression the child has is to bite his hand. Thus several factors have contributed to this one behaviour.

The range of possible causes for a specific behaviour can be illustrated by examining self-injurious behaviour. A very small minority of children and adults with autism deliberately injure themselves. They are usually those who are severely or profoundly intellectually disabled and often with poor means of communication. They may bang their heads on objects such as the floor, bite themselves, hit their head or body – often the upper chest – with their fist or scratch themselves.

Fortunately, such behaviour is a rare phenomenon but when it does occur it can be very distressing and there may be no obvious cause.

Having observed such behaviour and designed many treatment programmes I have identified three potential causes. The following screening method can be used to provide an explanation for the behaviour and a management strategy.

First question: is the behaviour due to pain?

Otitis media (earache) is a common cause of self-injury, particularly injuries to the head. Young children are prone to earache and, if this behaviour has never occurred before and there is a suspicion of a high temperature, infection, headache or pain, then ask a medical practitioner for their advice. The management strategy is then determined by the doctor. In this instance the behaviour is quite normal and occurs in many ordinary young children.

Second question: is the behaviour a means of communication?

If the behaviour is not a response to pain, then it could be a means of communication. If someone is unable effectively to communicate their thoughts and feelings by speech or gesture, the only alternative means they have is behaviour. Thus self-injury may be used as a means of communication.

Anne Donnellan and her colleagues have analysed the communicative function of aberrant behaviours such as self-injury and there are several potential translations, namely:[42]

- I want it now
- I don't understand
- I don't want to do this
- stop
- no
- leave me alone
- it's all too much

Careful observation of the person may indicate that the self-injury occurs in specific situations, often when the person with ASD is frustrated or under stress. Common situations which may lead to self-injury are when the person is thwarted in their demand for something, instructed to do an activity they do not want to do or there is too much noise, chaos or social demands.

Striking the forehead as a means of expressing exasperation is a natural gesture for us all. However, a person with ASD has difficulty expressing subtle emotions and when angry or distressed their feelings are usually expressed very physically and vividly. Thus, when a child is thwarted, for example if he cannot have the chocolate biscuit his classmate is eating, he bangs his forehead on the floor in frustration.

This behaviour is quite understandable given the unique disabilities found in ASD but the child may subsequently learn that by banging his head his teacher gives him what he wants in order to calm him down and stop him hurting himself. The behaviour then has a translation of 'I want it now' and becomes an effective means of blackmail.

The management strategy is to ensure that such behaviour is not allowed to be successful. You may try to distract him with some other activity or simply place a cushion between his head and the floor but don't give in.

Alternatively, self-injury may be due to frustration in situations where the person is unsure of what to do or knows he is likely to fail. The behaviour is a means of communicating 'I don't understand' or 'I don't want to do this'.

The management strategy is to recognise the person's apprehension and reluctance, offer reassurance, simplify the instructions and task, and provide more guidance and encouragement. Do not make any comment on failure or incompetence – just quietly show the correct way.

The behaviour may also translate to 'I would rather continue doing this.' In that case, assuming the activity you propose is necessary, provide reassurance that she can return to her previous activity or something else she likes doing when she has finished.

Self-injury can be an extremely effective means of communicating 'Stop', 'No' or 'I want a break'. If you notice that you have exhausted the attention span or tolerance of the person with ASD, then at this point – before they self-injure – teach him a sign, sound or gesture which indicates 'Finish' and end the activity. The person may then learn to use this alternative and more appropriate means of communicating 'I have had enough'.

The behaviour may translate to 'Leave me alone' or 'It's all too much'. People with ASD have a low tolerance of chaos, noise or social demands and may learn that by injuring themselves or other people they are sent outside, or to a secluded room, for example 'time out'. If the self-injury is a response to excessive stimulation or demands, then it is essential to try and reduce these before the injury begins. You may reduce the noise-level, offer some distracting solitary activity or actually encourage the person to take a 'five minute break' in a quiet corner to help them calm down.

Third question: is the behaviour due to an abnormality of brain physiology?

Over the last few years there has been increasing evidence from research studies that self-injurious behaviour that is not simply due to pain or used as a means of communication may be due to a dysfunction of brain biochemistry or epilepsy.

Some of the symptoms of ASD, especially social withdrawal, repetitive behaviour and insensitivity to pain, are also observed in people who are opiate addicts unable to maintain their addiction. The human body has a natural opiate system that has many functions, one of which is pain relief. There are now several theories which propose that in autism there is an abnormality of the natural opiate system.[110-112]

Self-injurious behaviour may be the means that people with ASD have of stimulating their dysfunctional opiate system. Certainly some children and adults with autism who self-injure do so regularly, often every few minutes, irrespective of any changes in their circumstances. They often have a strong determination to self-injure, with obvious annoyance when prevented. They also discover alternative means to self-injure, such as bending back their fingers. There has been some success in reducing the frequency and intensity of such self-injurious behaviour by administering drugs developed for use with heroin addicts during withdrawal but not all studies have been successful.[112-116]

A previous section explained how particular forms of epilepsy may affect a person's behaviour and that self-injurious behaviour has been attributed to complex partial seizures which originate in the frontal lobes of the brain.[104] These are sudden, unpredictable, and often intense outbursts of self-injury. If observation shows this particular pattern then the person should be referred to a neurologist.

The process of identifying the cause of a specific behaviour requires knowledge of ASD, access to a variety of professional skills and the collection of information by observation and discussion. It may take a while to find the reason for the behaviour but, once the reasons are known, then there are effective management techniques.

However, it may take time to identify the cause or for long-term strategies to take effect. In the meantime you may have to deal with someone whose behaviour is becoming increasingly difficult. The following is a sequence of strategies for dealing with increasing levels of agitated behaviour.

1. Identify any signals which indicate increased levels of stress.
2. Organise some distracting activity.
3. Encourage relaxation or vigorous physical activities to reduce the level of stress.
4. Impose verbal control.
5. Leave well alone.

Stage 1 Identify the signals of distress

A child or adult with ASD may have a unique way of expressing their increasing level of agitation. It may be by specific sounds, words, or actions. These can range from sudden squeaks and rocking to self-injury or repeating conversations that occurred during a similar situation, perhaps many years ago.

Stage 2 Organise some distracting activity

Once you have identified the signals of distress, try to distract the person's attention to some alternative routine activity, preferably something they are good at. Useful examples in the home are clearing the table or changing clothes. A simple procedure is to say 'Stop,' whatever the agitated behaviour is; then start some easy task; finally, if the person responds appropriately, thank them for complying with your request.

In such a situation you should avoid the word 'No' as from experience I have found that this one word can be a most provocative comment, leading to an increase in agitation. It is also important to avoid any criticism of the person as this can also inflame the situation. The idea is to simply turn their attention onto some easy task.

Stage 3 Relaxation or physical activities

But what if distraction does not work?

The next stage is to encourage the person to calm down either by relaxation or by 'burning off' agitation by vigorous physical activities.

There are a number of ways that relaxation, perhaps the first option, can be achieved. A quiet retreat or sanctuary may help. This can be the person's bedroom or a secluded and quiet area in the classroom or workplace. The intention is that the person should be temporarily away from the situation which caused the agitated behaviour. The secluded area should be comfortable, perhaps with music if this is a means of relaxation for that person.

Temple Grandin describes her own need for a sanctuary: 'All of us need a private place. Children with autism need their secret places, too, in which they can hide and retreat to their own world. After all, autism is a 'withinness' disability, and autistic children need the security of their own hideaways. I had mine and it was a place for me to think and recharge myself.' [91]

Specific relaxation techniques could be used, such as breath control and massage. These techniques should have first been used when the person with ASD was naturally calm so they are familiar with the procedures.

It may be possible to encourage the person to use their ritualistic behaviour as a means of diversion, and relaxation. Temple Grandin writes: 'my fixations reduced arousal and calmed me.'[91]

A recent conversation I had with a lady with Asperger syndrome included a discussion of her fascination with the Japanese tea ceremony. When I asked why, she replied that it helped her to relax. If a sanctuary is not available then a walk outside the building may help. All these techniques are designed to maintain the person's self-control and reduce the level of agitation or anxiety. When this has been achieved they must return to their previous activity. Otherwise they will quickly learn that disruptive behaviour can help avoid something they do not like.

There is increasing clinical and research evidence that regular physical exercise can have a very beneficial effect on the frequency of agitated behaviour in people with ASD.[117,118] The person with ASD may not be able to communicate effectively their increasing level of tension by verbal means with phrases such as 'I need a break' or non-verbal means such as gestures of exasperation. However, they can constructively reduce their level of tension by physical exercise.

This is much the same way as anyone 'blowing off steam' by playing a game of squash or mowing the lawn. The exercise can include aerobics, jogging or even using an exercise bike, trampoline or swing.[119-121] However, experience has shown these activities must be continuous, vigorous and for a minimum of 15 minutes.

One young man with ASD I saw recently was notorious for his outbursts of disruptive behaviour. We succeeded in reducing these significantly by noticing that when he became agitated he would increase the volume of his voice and start swearing at people. We then instructed him to go for a run around the perimeter of his residential unit. The route had been learnt previously by running with a member of staff and we knew he would keep to his specified route. Once he returned he made a tick on a special piece of paper on a noticeboard, indicating the number of runs he had each day. By his return he was invariably much calmer and more tolerant for the next hour or so.

There are also distinct advantages in such vigorous physical activities being dispersed throughout the person's day. The school can use activities in the hall or gym while the workplace can use the Japanese tradition of group physical exercise before and between work schedules. Indeed, this technique has been deliberately adopted in the curriculum of the Higashi Japanese School for children with autism in Boston.[122] Once the person has a regular opportunity to physically 'work out' their frustration or agitation, their subsequent level of tolerance noticeably improves. As Temple Grandin writes in her autobiography, 'Doing physical labour eased my nerve attacks.'[89]

Stage 4 Impose verbal control

Occasionally the self-control of the person with ASD may disintegrate and the situation deteriorates until someone imposes verbal control over the behaviour: in other words, verbally 'applying the brakes' to stop the behaviour.

In such circumstances the person in charge of the situation must impose their control in a firm, convincing and assertive way, using a simple but authoritative command such as 'Sit down'. There should be no ambiguity in the message or alternatives, either implicit or explicit. In such situations the person with ASD lacks and needs external control and you may have to be quite firm.

Stage 5 Leave well alone

If all the previous approaches have failed and the person with ASD is uncontrollable, then leave them alone, as to go close to console or restrain the person may put you at risk of being accidentally or deliberately hurt. This may cause the person with ASD to become even more distressed. In such circumstances, all you may be able to do is 'weather the storm' from a distance until the person finally calms down. However, should they become a danger to themselves or other people, then some form of restraint may be necessary.

When the person is calming down there are certain actions which may aggravate the situation and these are to be avoided. At this stage any ambiguous or sarcastic comments such as 'I hope you are pleased with yourself' may make you feel better but will really confuse the person with ASD. Any reference to consequences such as 'Well, no ice cream for you tonight' might prove equally provocative. The time to discuss consequences is when the person has completely returned to normal and can cope with the results of their behaviour.

In summary, if the level of agitated behaviour increases, there are a number of options available, depending on the severity of the behaviour.

- In the early stages, when the behaviour is fairly mild, use distraction, relaxation or physical activities.
- If this does not work then you may have to take control of the person's behaviour by assertive verbal means.
- If all the above fail, do not put yourself at risk but retire to a safe distance until the person eventually calms down.
- Remember not to precipitate another disruptive episode by prematurely imposing consequences or giving ambiguous messages.

Conclusion

This book should provide a better understanding of the unique disabilities associated with ASD and an explanation of how they cause such unusual behaviour. However, one must always remember that the answer to the question 'Why does Chris do that?' may not be due to a specific characteristic of ASD but simply that the behaviour is quite normal for a person of that age, or is just an expression of his or her personality.

One must also consider how the individual's personality affects the expression of ASD as some appear very distressed by their disability while others are extraordinarily tolerant. Nevertheless, all should be applauded for their courage.

ASD can produce times of exasperation but it can also produce times of achievement. It should not be considered a tragedy but a challenge. Recently so much has been discovered about the nature of ASD that we are becoming more able to provide an explanation of why such unusual behaviour occurs and, more importantly, ways to reduce its consequences on the person's behaviour, learning and social life.

References

[1] American Psychiatric Association. (2000). *Diagnostic and statistical manual of mental disorders* (4th ed., text revision). Washington, DC: Author.

[2] Gillberg, C. (1991). Clinical and neurobiological aspects of Asperger syndrome in six family studies. In Frith, U. (Ed.), *Autism and Asperger syndrome.* Cambridge: Cambridge University Press.

Attwood, T. (1998). *Asperger's syndrome: A guide for parents and professionals.* London: Jessica Kingsley.

[3] Baron-Cohen, S. (1989). Perceptual role taking and protodeclarative pointing in autism. *British Journal of Developmental Psychology, 7*, 113-127.

Attwood, T. (2000). Strategies for improving the social integration of children with Asperger Syndrome. *Autism, 4*, 85-100.

[4] Landry, S.H., and Loveland, K.A. (1989). The effect of social context on the functional communication skills of autistic children. *Journal of Autism and Developmental Disorders, 19*, 288-299.

Tjus, T., Heimann, and Nelson, K.E. (2001). Interaction patterns between children and their teachers when using a specific multimedia and communication strategy: Observations from children with autism and mixed intellectual disabilities. *Autism, 5*, 175-188.

[5] Sigman, M., Mundy, P., Sherman, T., and Ungerer, J. (1986). Social interactions of autistic, mentally retarded and normal children and their caregivers. *Journal of Child Psychology and Psychiatry, 27*, 647-656.

Paul, R. (2003). Promoting social communication in high functioning individuals with autistic spectrum disorders. *Child and Adolescent Psychiatric Clinics of North America, 12*, 87-106.

[6] Lord, C., and Hopkins, J.M. (1986). The social behaviour of autistic children with younger and same-age non-handicapped peers. *Journal of Autism and Developmental Disorders, 16*, 249-262.

Zercher, C., Hunt, P., Schuler, A., and Webster, J. (2001). Increasing joint attention, play and language through peer supported play. *Autism, 5*, 374-398.

[7] Brady, M.P., Shores, R.E., McEvoy, M.A., Ellis, D., and Fox, J.J. (1987). Increasing social interactions of severely handicapped autistic children. *Journal of Autism and Developmental Disorders, 17*, 375-390.

Kok, A.J., Kong, T.Y., and Bernard-Opitz, V. (2002). A comparison of the effects of structured play and facilitated play approaches on preschoolers with autism: a case study. *Autism, 6*, 181-196.

[8] Oke, J.N., and Schreibman, L. (1990). Training social initiations to a high-functioning autistic child: assessment of collateral behaviour change and generalization in a case study. *Journal of Autism and Developmental Disorders, 20*, 479-497.

Attwood, T. (2000). Strategies for improving the social integration of children with Asperger syndrome. *Autism, 4*, 85-100.

[9]Mesibov, G.B. (1984). Social skills training with verbal autistic adolescents and adults: a program model. *Journal of Autism and Developmental Disorders, 14,* 395-404.

Attwood, T. (2000). Strategies for improving the social integration of children with Asperger syndrome. *Autism, 4,* 85-100.

[10]Williams, T.I. (1989). A social skills group for autistic children. *Journal of Autism and Developmental Disorders, 19,* 143-155.

Paul, R. (2003). Promoting social communication in high functioning individuals with autistic spectrum disorders. *Child and Adolescent Psychiatric Clinics of North America, 12,* 87-106.

[11]Taras, M.E., Matson, J.L., and Leary, C. (1988). Training social interpersonal skills in two autistic children. *Journal of Behaviour Therapy and Experimental Psychiatry, 19,* 275-280.

Attwood, T. (2000). Strategies for improving the social integration of children with Asperger syndrome. *Autism, 4,* 85-100.

[12]Charlop, M.H., and Milstein, J.P. (1989). Teaching autistic children conversational speech using video modeling. *Journal of Applied Behavior Analysis, 22,* 275-28.

Schreibman, L., Whalen, C., and Stahmer, A.C. (2000). The use of video priming to reduce disruptive transition behavior in children with autism. *Journal of Positive Behavior Interventions, 2,* 3-11.

[13]Groden, J., and Cautela, J. (1988). Procedures to increase social interaction among adolescents with autism: A multiple baseline analysis. *Journal of Behaviour Therapy and Experimental Psychiatry, 19,* 87-93.

[14]Dewey, M. (1991). Living with Asperger's syndrome. In Frith, U. (Ed.), *Autism and Asperger syndrome.* Cambridge: Cambridge University Press.

[15]Frith, U. (1989). *Autism – Explaining the enigma.* Oxford: Basil Blackwell Limited.

Blackshaw, A.J., Kinderman, P., Hare, D.J. and Hatton, C. (2001). Theory of mind, causal attribution and paranoia in Asperger Syndrome. *Autism, 5,* 147-164.

[16]Baron-Cohen, S. (1990). Autism: A specific-cognitive disorder of 'mind-blindness'. International *Review of Psychiatry, 2,* 81-90.

Blackshaw, A.J., Kinderman, P., Hare, and Hatton, C. (2001). Theory of mind, causal attribution and paranoia in Asperger syndrome. *Autism, 5,* 135-146.

[17]Hobson, R.P. (1989). Beyond cognition: A theory of autism. In Dawson, G. (Ed.), *Autism – Nature, diagnosis, and treatment.* New York: The Guilford Press.

[18]Walters, A.S., Rowland, P. B., and Feinstein, C. (1990). Social relatedness and autism: Current research, issues, directions. *Research in Developmental Disabilities, 11,* 303-326.

[19]Tantam, D., Monaghan, L., Nicholson, H., and Stirling, J. (1989). Autistic children's ability to interpret faces: A research note. *Journal of Child Psychology and Psychiatry, 30,* 623-630.

Attwood, T. (2000). Strategies for improving the social integration of children with Asperger syndrome. *Autism, 4,* 85-100.

[20]Hobson, R.P. (1986). The autistic child's appraisal of expressions of emotion. *Journal of Child Psychology and Psychiatry, 27,* 321-342.

Dennis, M., Lockyer, L., and Lazenby, A.L. (2000). How high-functioning children with autism understand real and receptive emotions. *Autism, 4,* 370-382.

[21]Hobson, R.P., Ouston, J., and Lee A. (1988). Emotion recognition in autism: Coordinating faces and voices. *Psychological Medicine, 18,* 911-923.

Nadel, J., Crove, S., Mattlinger, M.J., Canet, P., Hudelot, Lecuyer, C., and Martini, M. (2000). Do children with autism have expectancies about the social behaviour of unfamiliar people? A pilot study using the still face paradigm. *Autism, 4,* 133-146.

[22] Wing, L., and Attwood, A. (1987). *Syndromes of autism and atypical development: Handbook of autism and pervasive developmental disorders*. New York: John Wiley and Sons.

Quill, K. A. (2000). *Do-watch-listen-say: Social and communication intervention for children with autism*. Baltimore, MD: Brookes.

[23] Langdell, T. (1981). *Face perception: An approach to the study of autism*. Ph.d. Thesis. University of London.

Dennis, M., Lockyer, L., and Lazenby, A.L. (2000). How high-functioning children with autism understand real and deceptive emotion. *Autism, 4*, 370-381.

[24] Macdonald, H., Rutter, M., Howlin, P., Rios, P., Le Couteur, A., Evered C., and Folstein, S. (1989). Recognition and expression of emotional cues by autistic and normal adults. *Journal of Child Psychology and Psychiatry, 30*, 6, 865-877.

Nadel, J., Crove, S., Mattlinger, M.J., Canet, P., Hudelot, Lecuyer, C., and Martini, M. (2000). Do children with autism have expectancies about the social behaviour of unfamiliar people? A pilot study using the still face paradigm. *Autism, 4*, 133-146.

[25] Attwood, A.J., Frith, U., and Hermelin, B. (1988). The understanding and use of interpersonal gestures by autistic and Down's syndrome children. *Journal of Autism and Developmental Disorders, 18*, 241-257.

[26] McEvoy, M.A., Nordquist, V.M., Twardosz, Heekaman, K.A., Wehby J., and Kenton, D. (1988). Promoting autistic children's peer interaction in an integrated early childhood setting using affection activities. *Journal of Applied Behavior Analysis, 21*, 193-200.

Odom, S.L., McConnell, S.R., McEvoy, M.A., Peterson, C., Ostrosky, M., and Chandler, L.K (1999). Relative effects of interventions for supporting the social competence of young children with disabilities. *Topics in Early Childhood Special Education, 19*, 75-92.

[27] Klin, A. (1991). Young autistic children's listening preferences in regard to speech: A possible characterization of the symptom of social withdrawal. *Journal of Autism and Developmental Disorders, 21*, 29-42.

Wetherby, A.M., and Prizant, B.M. (2000). *Autism spectrum disorders: A transactional developmental perspective*. Baltimore, MD: Paul H. Brookes Publishing Company.

[28] Williams, T.I. (1990). Language acquisition in autistic children: A research note. *European Journal of Psychiatry, 4*, 173-179.

Wetherby, A.M., and Prizant, B.M. (2000). *Autism spectrum disorders: A transactional developmental perspective*. Baltimore, MD: Paul H. Brookes Publishing Company.

[29] Howlin, P. (1989). Changing approaches to communication training with autistic children. *British Journal of Disorders of Communication, 24*, 151-161.

Frea, W.D., Arnold, C.L., and Vittimberga, G.L. (2001). A demonstration of the effects of augmentative communication on the extreme aggressive behavior of a child with autism within an integrated preschool setting. *Journal of Positive Behavior Interventions, 3*, 194-198.

[30] Rutter, M., and Schopler, E. (1987). Autism and pervasive developmental disorders: Concepts and diagnostic issues. *Journal of Autism and Developmental Disorders, 17*, 159-186.

Klin, A., and Volkmar, F.R. (2003). Asperger syndrome: Diagnosis and external validity. *Child and Adolescent Psychiatric Clinics of North America, 12*, 1-14.

[31] McGee, G.G., Krantz, J., Mason, D., and McClannahan, L.E. (1983). A modified incidental teaching procedure for autistic youth: acquisition and generalisation of receptive object labels. *Journal of Applied Behavior Analysis, 16*, 329-338.

Galensky, R.L., Miltenberger, R.G., Stricker, J.M., and Garlinghouse, M.A. (2001). Functional assessment and treatment of mealtime behavior problems. *Journal of Positive Behavior Interventions, 3*, 211-224.

[32] Prizant, B., and Wetherby, A. (1985). Intentional communicative behaviour of children with autism: theoretical and practical issues. *Australian Journal of Human Communication Disorders, 13*, 25-65.

Wetherby, A.M., and Prizant, B.M. (2000). *Autism spectrum disorders: A transactional developmental perspective*. Baltimore, MD: Paul H. Brookes Publishing Company.

[33] Datlow Smith, M., and Coleman, D. (1986). Managing the behaviour of adults with autism in the job setting. *Journal of Autism and Developmental Disorders, 16*, 145-154.

[34] Volden, J., and Lord, C. (1991). Neologisms and idiosyncratic language in autistic speakers. *Journal of Autism and Developmental Disorders, 21*, 109-130.

Wetherby, A.M., and Prizant, B.M. (2000). *Autism spectrum disorders: A transactional developmental perspective*. Baltimore, MD: Paul H. Brookes Publishing Company.

[35] Rutter, M. (1978). Diagnosis and definition. In M. Rutter and E. Schopler (Eds.), *Autism: A reappraisal of concepts and treatment*. New York: Plenum Press.

[36] Kiernan, C. (1983). The use of non-vocal communication systems with autistic individuals. *Journal of Child Psychology and Psychiatry, 24*, 339-376.

Wetherby, A.M., and Prizant, B.M. (2000). *Autism spectrum disorders: A transactional developmental perspective*. Baltimore, MD: Paul H. Brookes Publishing Company.

[37] De Villiers, J.G., and Naughton. (1974). Teaching a symbol language to autistic children. *Journal of Consulting and Clinical Psychology, 42*, 111-117.

Stiebel, D. (1999). Promoting augmentative communication during daily routines: A parent problem-solving routines. *Journal of Positive Behavior Interventions, 1*, 139-169.

[38] Lancioni, G.E. (1983). Using pictorial representations as communication means with low-functioning children. *Journal of Autism and Developmental Disorders, 13*, 87-105.

Frea, W.D., Arnold, C.L., and Vittimberga, G.L. (2001). A demonstration of the effects of augmentative communication on the extreme aggressive behavior of a child with autism within an integrated preschool setting. *Journal of Positive Behavior Interventions, 3*, 194-198.

[39] Berkowitz, S., (1990). A comparison of two methods of prompting in training discrimination of communication book pictures by autistic students. *Journal of Autism and Developmental Disorders, 20*, 255-262.

Wetherby, A.M., and Prizant, B.M. (2000). *Autism spectrum disorders: A transactional developmental perspective*. Baltimore, MD: Paul H. Brookes Publishing Company.

[40] Howlin, P., and Rutter, M. with Berger, M., Hemsley, R., Hersov, L., and Yule, W. (1987). *Treatment of autistic children*. Chichester: John Wiley.

[41] Biklen, D., Morton, M., Saha, S., Duncan J., Gold, D., Hardardottir, M., Karna, E., O'Connor, S., and Rao, S. (1991). 'I'm not autistic on the typewriter'. *Disability, Handicap and Society, 6*, 161-180.

[42] Donnellan, A.M., Mirenda, P.L., Mesaros, R.A., and Fassbender, L.L. (1984). Analyzing the communicative functions of aberrant behaviour. *Journal of the Association for Persons with Severe Handicaps, 9*, 201-212.

Blair, K.S., Umbreit, J., and Eck, S. (2000). Analysis of multiple variables related to a young child's aggressive behavior, *Journal of Positive Behavior Interventions, 2*, 33-39.

[43] Durand, Y.M., and Carr, E.G. (1987). Social influences on 'self-stimulatory' behaviour: analysis and treatment application. *Journal of Applied Behavior Analysis, 20*, 119-132.

Baker, M.J. (2000). Incorporating the thematic ritualistic behaviors of children with autism into games increasing social play interactions with siblings. *Journal of Positive Behavior Interventions, 2*, 66-84.

[44] Durand, Y.M., and Crimmins, D.B. (1987). Assessment and treatment of psychotic speech in an autistic child. *Journal of Autism and Developmental Disorders, 17*, 17-28.

Carr, E.G., Dunlap, G., Horner, R.H., Koegel, R.L., Turnbull, A.P., Sailor, W., Anderson, J.L., Albin, R.W., Koegel, L.K., and Fox, L. (2002). Positive behavior support: evolution of an applied science. *Journal of Positive Behavior Interventions, 4*, 4-16.

[45] Frankel, F., Simmons, J., Fichter, M., and Freeman, B.J. (1984). Stimulus overselectivity in autistic and mentally retarded children: a research note. *Journal of Child Psychology and Psychiatry, 25*, 147-155.

Wetherby, A.M., and Prizant, B.M. (2000). *Autism spectrum disorders: A transactional developmental perspective.* Baltimore, MD: Paul H. Brookes Publishing Company.

[46] Martineau, J., Garreau, B., Roux, S., and Lelord, G. (1987). Auditory evoked responses and their modifications during conditioning paradigm in autistic children. *Journal of Autism and Developmental Disorders, 17*, 525-539.

Roberts-Gwinn, M.M., Luiten, L., Derby, K.M., Johnson, T.A., and Weber, K. (2001). Identification of competing reinforcers for behavior maintained by automatic reinforcement. *Journal of Positive Behavior Interventions, 3*, 83-87, 94.

[47] Hermelin, B. (1978). Images and language. In M. Rutter, and E. Schopler (Eds.), *Autism: A reappraisal of concepts and treatment.* New York: Plenum Press.

Quill, K.A. (2000). Do-watch-listen-say: *Social and communication intervention for children with autism.* Baltimore, MD: Brookes.

[48] Ohta, M. (1987). Cognitive disorders of infantile autism: A study employing the WISC, spatial relationship conceptualization, and gesture imitations. *Journal of Autism and Developmental Disorders, 17*, 45-62.

Maurice, C., Green, F., and Luce S.C. (1996). *Behavioral intervention for young children with autism: A manual for parents and professionals.* Austin, TX: Pro-Ed, Inc.

[49] Datlow Smith, M. (1985). Managing the aggressive and self-injurious behaviour of adults disabled by autism. *Journal of the Association for Persons with Severe Handicaps 10*, 228-232.

Mesibov, G.B., Browder, D.M., and Kirkland, C. (2002). Using individualized schedules as a component of positive behavioral supports for students with developmental disabilities. *Journal of Positive Behavior Interventions*, 73-79.

[50] Baron-Cohen, S. (1987). Autism and symbolic play. *British Journal of Developmental Psychology, 5,* 139-148.

Nuzzolo-Gomez, R., Leonard, M.A., Ortiz, E., Rivera, C.M., and Greer, R.D. (2002). Teaching children with autism to prefer books or toys over stereotypy or passivity. *Journal of Positive Behavior Interventions, 4,* 80-87.

[51] Lewis, V., and Boucher, J. (1988). Spontaneous, instructed and elicited play in relatively able autistic children. *British Journal of Developmental Psychology, 6,* 325-339.

Zercher, C., Hunt, P., Schuler, A., and Webster, J. (2001). Increasing joint attention, play, and language through peer supported play. *Autism, 5,* 374-398.

[52] Newsone, E. (1991). *Enabling flexibility and social empathy in able autistic children: Some practical strategies.* Paper presented at Therapeutic Approaches to Autism – Research and Practise, Durham, U.K.

[53] Koegel, R.L., and Koegel, L.K. (1987). Generalisation issues in the treatment of autism. *Seminars in Speech and Language, 8,* 241-256.

Esbensade, P.H., and Rosales-Ruiz, J. (2001). Programming common stimuli to promote generalized question-asking: A case demonstration in a child with autism. *Journal of Positive Behavior Interventions, 3,* 199-210.

[54] Rotholz, D.A. (1987). Current considerations on the use of one-to-one instruction with autistic students: Review and recommendations. *Education and Treatment of Children, 10,* 271-278.

Kok, A.J., Kong, T.Y., and Bernard-Opitz, V. (2002). A comparison of the effects of structured play and facilitated play approaches on preschoolers with autism: A case study. *Autism, 6,* 181-196.

[55] Wing, L. (1967). The handicaps of autistic children. In B. Richards (Ed.), *Proceedings of the Congress of the International Association for the Scientific Study of Mental Deficiency.* England: Sidgwick and Jackson.

[56] Frith, U., and Baron-Cohen, S. (1987). Perception in autistic children. In D. Cohen and A.M. Donnellan (Eds.), *Handbook of autism and pervasive developmental disorders.* New York: John Wiley.

Dunn, W., Myles, B.S., and Orr, S. (2002). Sensory processing issues associated with Asperger Syndrome: A preliminary investigation. *The American Journal of Occupational Therapy, 56,* 97-102.

[57] Hamines, J.G.W., and Langdell, T. (1981). Precursors of symbol formation and childhood autism. *Journal of Autism and Developmental Disorders, 11,* 331-346.

National Research Council. (2001). *Educating children with autism.* Washington, DC: National Academy Press.

[58] Attwood, A.J. (1984). *The gestures of autistic children.* Unpublished Ph.D thesis, University of London, England.

[59] Riguet, C.B., Taylor, N.D, Benaroya, S., and Klein, L.S. (1981). Symbolic play in autistic, Down's and normal children of equivalent mental age. *Journal of Autism and Developmental Disorders, 11,* 439-448.

National Research Council. (2001). *Educating children with autism.* Washington, DC: National Academy Press.

[60] Stone, W.L., and Lemanek, K.L. (1990). Parental report of social behaviours in autistic preschoolers. *Journal of Autism and Developmental Disorders, 20,* 513-522.

Stone, W.L., and Yoder, P.J. (2001). Predicting spoken language level in children with autism spectrum disorders. *Autism, 5,* 341-361.

[61]Dawson, G., and Levy, A. (1989). Arousal, attention, and the socioemotional impairments of individuals with autism. In G. Dawson (Ed.), *Autism – Nature, diagnosis, and treatment*. New York: The Guilford Press.

[62]Wing, L. (1976). Diagnosis, clinical description and prognosis. In L. Wing (Ed.), *Early childhood autism*. Oxford: Pergamon.

[63]Grandin, T. (1984). My experiences as an autistic child and review of selected literature. *Journal of Orthomolecular Psychiatry, 13*, 144-174.

Quill, K. A. (2000). *Do-watch-listen-say: Social and communication intervention for children with autism*. Baltimore, MD: Brookes.

[64]Boucher, J., and Lewis, V. (1989). Memory impairments and communication in relatively able autistic children. *Journal of Child Psychology and Psychiatry, 30*, 99-122.

Frea, W.D., Arnold, C.L., and Vittimberga, G.L. (2001). A demonstration of the effects of augmentative communication on the extreme aggressive behavior of a child with autism within an integrated preschool setting. *Journal of Positive Behavior Interventions, 3*, 194-198.

[65]Atkinson, R.P., Jenson, W.R., Rovner, L., Cameron, S., Van Wagenen, and Petersen, B.P. (1984). Brief report: Validation of the autism reinforcer checklist for children. *Journal of Autism and Developmental Disorders, 14*, 429-433.

[66]Baker, L., and Milner, Y. (1985). Sensory reinforcement with autistic children. *Behavioral Psychology, 13*, 328-341.

Kennedy, C.H. (2000). When reinforcers for problem behavior are not readily apparent: Extending functional assessments to complex problem behaviors. *Journal of Positive Behavior Interventions, 2*, 195-201.

[67]Charlop, M.H., Kurtz, P.E., and Casey, E.G. (1990). Using aberrant behaviours as reinforcers for autistic children. *Journal of Applied Behavior Analysis, 23*, 163-181.

Baker, M.J., Koegel, R.L., and Koegel, L.K. (1998). Increasing the social behavior of young children with autism using their obsessions. *Journal of the Association for Persons of Severe Handicaps, 23*, 300-309.

[68]Dyer, K., Christian, W.P., and Luce, S.C. (1982). The role of response delay in improving the discrimination performance of autistic children. *Journal of Applied Behavior Analysis, 15*, 231-240.

Quill, K. A. (2000). *Do-watch-listen-say: Social and communication intervention for children with autism*. Baltimore, MD: Brookes.

[69]Hughes, V., Wolery, M.R., and Neel, R.S. (1988). Teacher verbalizations and task performance with autistic children. *Journal of Autism and Developmental Disorders, 13*, 305-316.

National Research Council. (2001). *Educating children with autism*. Washington, DC: National Academy Press.

[70]Koegel, R.L., O'Dell, M., and Dunlap, G. (1988). Producing speech use in non-verbal autistic children by reinforcing attempts. *Journal of Autism and Developmental Disorders, 18*, 525-538.

[71]Dunlap, G., and Koegel R.L. (1980). Motivating autistic children through stimulus variation. *Journal of Applied Behavior Analysis, 13*, 619-627.

Quill, K. A. (2000). *Do-watch-listen-say: Social and communication intervention for children with autism*. Baltimore, MD: Brookes.

[72]De Myer, M.K. (1979). *Parents and children in autism*. Washington, DC: Winston.

[73] Tantam, D. (1991). Asperger syndrome in adulthood. In U. Frith. (Ed.), *Autism and Asperger syndrome*. Cambridge: Cambridge University Press.

Tantam, D. (2003). The challenge of adolescents and adults with Asperger syndrome. *Child and Adolescent Psychiatric Clinics of North America, 12*, 143-164.

[74] Baron-Cohen, S. (1989). Do autistic children have obsessions and compulsions? *British Journal of Clinical Psychology, 28*, 193-200.

American Psychiatric Association. (2000). *Diagnostic and statistical manual of mental disorders – 4th ed., text revision*. Washington, DC: Author.

[75] Barmann B.C. (1980) Use of contingent vibration in the treatment of self- stimulatory hand-mouthing and ruminative vomiting behaviour. *Journal of Behavioural Therapy and Experimental Psychiatry, 11*, 307-311.

Kennedy, C.H. (2000). When reinforcers for problem behavior are not readily apparent: Extending functional assessments to complex problem behaviors. *Journal of Positive Behavior Interventions, 2*, 195-201.

[76] Haring, T.G., Pitts-Conway, V., Breen, C.G., and Gaylord-Ross, R. (1986). Use of differential reinforcement of other behaviour during dyadic instruction to reduce stereotyped behavior of autistic students. *American Journal of Mental Deficiency, 90*, 694-702.

Roberts-Gwinn, M.M., Luiten, L., Derby, K.M., Johnson, T.A., and Weber, K. (2001). Identification of competing reinforcers for behavior maintained by automatic reinforcement. *Journal of Positive Behavior Interventions, 3*, 83-87, 94.

[77] Koegel, R.L., and Koegel, L.K. (1990). Extended reductions in stereotypic behaviour of students with autism through a self-management treatment package. *Journal of Applied Behavior Analysis, 23*, 119-127.

Callahan, K., and Rademacher, J.A. (1999). Using self-management strategies to increase the on-task behavior of a student with autism, *Journal of Positive Behavior Interventions, 1*, 117-122.

[78] Runco, M.A., Charlop, M.H., and Schreibman, L. (1986). The occurrence of autistic children's self-stimulation as a function of familiar versus unfamiliar stimulus conditions. *Journal of Autism and Developmental Disorders, 16*, 31-44.

Huebner, R.A. (2001). *Autism: A sensorimotor approach to management*. Gaithersburg, MD: Aspen Publishers, Inc.

[79] Dadds, M., Schwarz, S., Adams, T., and Rose, S. (1988). The effects of social context and verbal skill on the stereotypic and task-involved behaviour of autistic children. *Journal of Child Psychology and Psychiatry, 29*, 669-676.

[80] Duker, P.C., and Rasing, E. (1989). Effects of redesigning the physical environment on self-stimulation and on-task behaviour in three autistic-type developmentally disabled individuals. *Journal of Autism and Developmental Disorders, 19*, 449-460.

Kennedy, C.H. (2000). When reinforcers for problem behavior are not readily apparent: Extending functional assessments to complex problem behaviors. *Journal of Positive Behavior Interventions, 2*, 195-201.

[81] Bemporad, J.R. (1979). Adult recollections of a formerly autistic child. *Journal of Autism and Developmental Disorders, 9*, 179-197.

[82] James, A.L., and Barry, R.J. (1980). Respiratory and vascular responses to simple visual stimuli in autistics, retardates and normals. *Psychophysiology, 17*, 541-547.

Huebner, R.A. (2001). *Autism: A sensorimotor approach to management*. Gaithersburg, MD: Aspen Publishers, Inc.

[83] Courchesne, E., and Lincoln, A.J., (1985). Event-related brain potential correlates of the processing of novel visual and auditory information in autism. *Journal of Autism and Developmental Disorders, 15*, 55-76.

[84] Ornitz, E.M. (1989). Autism at the interface between sensory and information processing. In G. Dawson (Ed.), *Autism – Nature, diagnosis and treatment.* New York: The Guilford Press.

[85] Coleman, M., and Gillberg C. (1985). *The biology of the autistic syndrome.* Oxford: Mac Keith Press.

Coleman, M., and Gillberg C. (2000). *The biology of the autistic syndrome (3rd ed.).* Oxford: Mac Keith Press.

[86] Gillberg, C. (1990). Autism under age 3 years: A clinical study of 28 cases referred for autistic symptoms in infancy. *Journal of Child Psychology and Psychiatry, 31*, 921-934.

Huebner, R.A. (2001). *Autism: A sensorimotor approach to management.* Gaithersburg, MD: Aspen Publishers, Inc.

[87] Frith, U. (1991). Asperger and his syndrome. In U. Frith (Ed.), *Autism and Asperger syndrome.* Cambridge: Cambridge University Press.

Dunn, W. (1999). *The sensory profile.* San Antonio, TX: The Psychological Corporation.

[88] Lowdon, G. (1991). Some thoughts on the nature of perception in autism. *Communication, 25*, 21-24.

Dunn, W. (1999). *The sensory profile.* San Antonio, TX: The Psychological Corporation.

[89] White, B.B., and White, M.S. (1987). Autism from the inside. *Medical Hypotheses, 24*, 223-229.

[90] Volkmar, F.R., and Cohen, D.J. (1985). The experience of infantile autism: A first-person account by Tony W. *Journal of Autism and Developmental Disorders, 15*, 47-54.

[91] Grandin, T., and Scariano, M. (1986). *Emergence: Labeled autistic.* Novato, CA: Arena Press.

[92] Cesaroni, L., and Garber, M. (1991). Exploring the experience of autism through firsthand accounts. *Journal of Autism and Developmental Disorders, 21*, 303-313.

[93] Grandin, T. (1989). An autistic's view of holding therapy. *Communication, 23*, 75-78.

[94] Grandin, T. (1990). Sensory problems in autism. In *Proceedings of the Annual Conference of the Autism Society of America*, Buena Park, California.

[95] Ram, S. (1990). The use of the duvet (quilt) for the treatment of autistic, violent behaviours (an experimental account). *Journal of Autism and Developmental Disorders, 20*, 279-280.

[96] King, L.J. (1990). Methods for reducing hypersensitivity to sensory stimulation in autistic individuals. *Proceedings of Autism Society Conference*, Buena Park, California.

Roberts-Gwinn, M.M., Luiten, L., Derby, K.M., Johnson, T.A., and Weber, K. (2001). Identification of competing reinforcers for behavior maintained by automatic re-inforcement. *Journal of Positive Behavior Interventions, 3*, 83-87, 94.

[97] Love, S.R., Matson, J.L., and West, D. (1990). Mothers as effective therapists for autistic children's phobias. *Journal of Applied Behavior Analysis, 23*, 379-385.

[98] Jackson, H.J. (1983). Current trends in the treatment of phobias in autistic and mentally retarded persons. *Australia and New Zealand Journal of Developmental Disabilities, 9*, 191-208.

[99] Waranch, H.R., Wohl, M.K., and Nidiffer, F.D. (1981). Treatment of a retarded adult's mannequin phobia through in vivo desensitization and shaping approach responses. *Journal of Behaviour Therapy and Experimental Psychiatry, 12*, 359-362.

[100] Gillberg, C., and Schaumann, H. (1989). Autism: Specific problems of adolescence. In C. Gillberg, (Ed.), *Diagnosis and treatment of autism.* New York: Plenum Press.

Attwood, T. (1998). *Asperger's syndrome: A guide for parents and professionals.* London: Jessica Kingsley.

[101] Gillberg, C. (1984). Autistic children growing up: Problems during puberty and adolescence. *Developmental Medicine and Child Neurology, 26*, 125-129.

Attwood, T. (1998). *Asperger's syndrome: A guide for parents and professionals.* London: Jessica Kingsley.

[102] Gillberg, C. (1990). The treatment of epilepsy in autism. *Journal of Autism and Developmental Disorders, 21*, 61-77.

Tuchman, R. (2000). Treatment of seizure disorders and EEG abnormalities of children with autism spectrum disorders. *Journal of Autism and Developmental Disorders, 30*, 137-148.

[103] Olsson, I., Steffenburg, S., and Gillberg, C. (1988). Epilepsy in autism and autistic like conditions. *Archives of Neurology, 45*, 666-668.

Kanner, A.M. (2000). The treatment of seizure disorders and EEG abnormalities in children with autistic spectrum disorders: Are we getting ahead of ourselves. *Journal of Autism and Developmental Disorders, 30*, 491-495.

[104] Gedye, A. (1989). Extreme self-injury attributed to frontal lobe seizures. *American Journal on Mental Retardation, 94*, 20-26.

[105] Szatmari, P., Bartolucci, G., Bremner, R., Bond, S., and Rich, S. (1989). A follow-up study of high-functioning autistic children. *Journal of Autism and Developmental Disorders, 19*, 213-225.

Attwood, T. (1998). *Asperger's syndrome: A guide for parents and professionals.* London: Jessica Kingsley.

[106] Gillberg, C. (1991). Outcome in autism and autistic-like conditions. *Journal of the American Academy of Adolescent and Child Psychiatry, 30*, 375-382.

Coleman, M., and Gillberg C. (2000). *The biology of the autistic syndrome (3rd ed.).* Oxford: Mac Keith Press.

[107] Wing, L. (1989). Autistic adults. In C. Gillberg (Ed.), *Diagnosis and treatment of autism.* New York: Plenum Press.

[108] Tantam, D. (1988). Lifelong eccentricity and social isolation. *British Journal of Psychiatry, 153*, 777-782.

Tantam, D. (2003). The challenge of adolescents and adults with Asperger syndrome. *Child and Adolescent Psychiatric Clinics of North America, 12*, 143-164.

[109] Szatmari, P., Bartolucci, G., and Bremner, R. (1989). Asperger's syndrome and autism: Comparison of early history and outcome. *Developmental Medicine and Child Neurology, 31*, 709-720.

Tonge, B.J., Brereton, A.V., Gray, K.M., and Einfeld, W.L. (1999). Behavioral and emotional disturbance in high-functioning autism and Asperger syndrome. *Autism, 3*, 117-130.

[110] Sahley, T.L., and Panksepp, J. (1987). Brain opioids and autism: An updated analysis of possible linkages. *Journal of Autism and Developmental Disorders, 17*, 201-216.

[111] Gillberg, C. (1988). The role of the endogenous opioids in autism and possible relationships to clinical features. *Aspects of Autism: Biological Research.* London: Gaskell.

[112] Sandman, C.A. (1988). B-Endorphin disregulation in autistic and self-injurious behaviour: A neuro-developmental hypothesis. *Synapse, 2,* 193-199.

[113] Campbell, M., Adarns, P., Small, A.M., Tesch, R.N., and Curren, E.L. (1988). Naltrexone in infantile autism. *Psychopharmacology Bulletin, 24,* 135-139.

[114] Barrett, R.P., Feinstein C., and Hole, W.T. (1989). Effects of Naloxone and Naltrexone on self-injury: A double-blind, placebo-controlled analysis. *American Journal on Mental Retardation, 93,* 644-651.

[115] Waiters, A., Barrett, R., Feinstein, C., Mercurio, A., and Hole, W. (1990). A case report of naltrexone treatment of self-injury and social withdrawal in autism. *Journal of Autism and Developmental Disorders, 20,* 169-176.

[116] Luiselli, J.K., Beitis, J.A., and Bass, J. (1989). Clinical analysis of Naltrexone in the treatment of self-injurious behaviour. *Journal of the Multihandicapped Person, 2,* 43-50.

[117] Rimland, B. (1990). Autism therapies from A to Z: Consumer report evaluations of treatment modalities. In *Proceedings 1990 Annual Conference of the Autism Society of America,* Buena Park, California.

Rosenthal-Malek, A., and Mitchell, S. (1997). Brief report: The effects of exercise on the self-stimulatory behaviors and positive responding to adolescents with autism. *Journal and Autism and Developmental Disorders, 27,* 193-201.

[118] Allison, D.B., Basile, V.C., and Macdonald, R.B. (1991). Comparative effects of antecedent exercise and Lorazepam on the aggressive behaviour of an autistic man. *Journal of Autism and Developmental Disorders, 21,* 89-94.

Elliot, R.O., Dobbin, A.R., Rose, G.D., and Soper, N.V. (1994). Vigorous, aerobic exercise versus general motor training activities: Effects on maladaptive and stereotypic behaviors of adults with both autism and mental retardation. *Journal of Autism and Developmental Disorders, 24,* 565-576.

[119] McGimsey, J.F., and Favell, (1988). The effects of increased physical exercise on disruptive behaviour in retarded persons. *Journal of Autism and Developmental Disorders, 18,* 167-179.

[120] Kern, L. Koegel, R.L., Dyer, K., Blew, P.A., and Fenton, L.R. (1982). The effects of physical exercise on self-stimulation and appropriate responding in autistic children. *Journal of Autism and Developmental Disorders, 12,* 399-419.

[121] Reid, R.D., Factor, D.C., Freeman, N.L., and Sherman, J. (1988). The effects of physical exercise on three autistic and developmentally disordered adolescents. *Therapeutic Recreation Journal, 22,* 47-56.

[122] Quill, K., Gurry, S., and Larkin, A. (1989). Daily life therapy: A Japanese model for educating children with autism. *Journal of Autism and Developmental Disorders, 19,* 625-635.

Honda, H., and Shimizu, Y. (2002). Early intervention for preschool children with autism in the community: The DISCOVERY approach in Yokohama, Japan, *Autism, 6,* 299-314.

Index

Other NAS titles published by AAPC include:

- *Asperger Syndrome – Practical Strategies for the Classroom: A Teacher's Guide* by Leicester City Council and Leicestershire County Council

- *Challenging Behaviour and Autism: Making Sense – Making Progress: A Guide to Preventing and Managing Challenging Behaviour for Parents and Teachers* by Philip Whitaker, Helen Joy, Jane Harley and David Edwards

- *Everybody Is Different: A Book for Young People Who Have Brothers or Sisters with Autism* by Fiona Bleach

- *It Can Get Better . . . Dealing with Common Behaviour Problems in Young Autistic Children: A Guide for Parents and Caregivers* by Paul Dickinson and Liz Hannah

- *The Other Half of Asperger Syndrome* by Maxine C. Aston

- *Teaching Young Children with Autistic Spectrum Disorders to Learn: A Practical Guide for Parents and Staff in General Education Classrooms and Preschools* by Liz Hannah

- *What Is Asperger Syndrome, and How Will It Affect Me? A Guide for Young People* by Martin Ives of the NAS Autism Helpline

- *Autism: How to Help Your Young Child* by Leicestershire County Council and Fosse Health Trust